Success in Maths

Rowena Onions
Chris Onions
Jacqueline Pendergast
Garry Pendergast
Series Editor: Jayne de Courcy

Ages 9–11

BOOK **3**

Contents

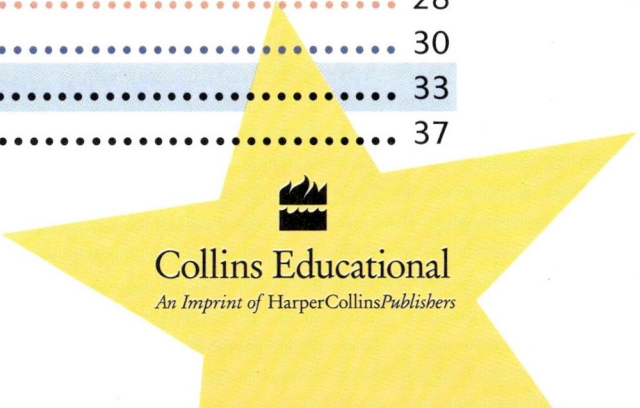

Collins Educational
An Imprint of HarperCollinsPublishers

The ⭐3 Steps to Success...

Step 1

Key skills practice

★ *Success in Maths Book 3* provides practice in a number of important Maths skills. These skills, which are developed further in Book 4, are the ones that your child needs to master in order to achieve a high level in the Maths National Test at the end of Key Stage 2. This book builds on the skills covered in *Success in Maths Books 1* and *2*.

★ Each chapter takes one Maths skill and gives your child practice in it, using graded questions. Your child should write the answers, with working where necessary, on separate sheets of paper.

★ This in-depth practice ensures that your child achieves real understanding of each skill.

Step 2

Practice with National Test Questions

★ The book contains three sections of *National Test Questions*. These questions have been included to test the skills covered in the chapters.

★ Your child can do these Test questions immediately after working on the skills chapters. You might, however, prefer to wait and ask your child to do them a little later to check that the topics have been thoroughly mastered.

Step 3

Improving your child's performance

★ The book contains detailed *Answers and Guidance* to both the skills practice questions and the *National Test Questions*.

★ The authors, who are KS2 Test Examiners, provide detailed guidance, showing how to go about answering the questions in the best possible way.

★ In this way, you can work with your child to improve both skills and performance in the KS2 Maths National Test.

Help with timing

★ As the Maths National Test papers are timed, it is important that your child learns to answer questions within a time limit.

★ Each skills chapter and each *Test Question* section gives target times for answering the questions. If you choose to, you can ask your child to time how long it takes to answer the questions. You can then compare your child's time against the target times provided. In this way, you will form a good idea of whether your child is working at the right rate to complete the Maths National Test papers successfully.

timed tests – Sha

Progression

★ *Success in Maths* is aimed at 9–11-year-olds who are in Years 5 and 6 of primary school. There is in-built progression: each book builds on skills covered in previous books.

★ To get the most out of *Success in Maths*, it is important that your child works through all four books in sequence. If you are buying this series for your child who is aged 9/10 (Year 5), then buy Books 1 and 2, and Books 3 and 4 at age 10/11 (Year 6). If your child is already in Year 6, then it is still advisable to work through from Book 1 to Book 4, to ensure that your child benefits from the progression built into the series.

Note to teachers

★ This book, and the other five titles in the *Success in Maths* series, are designed for use at home and in schools in Years 5 and 6. They focus on the key Maths skills that will raise children's performance in the Maths National Test.

★ You can use the books in class or give them to children for homework to ensure that they are fully prepared for their Maths National Test.

1 Multiplication and division by 10, 100, 1000 ...

What's it all about?

★ This chapter gives you practice in multiplying and dividing by orders of 10. **Write your answers on a separate sheet of paper, showing your working.**

★ Some of the questions ask you to use multiplication and division to solve everyday problems.

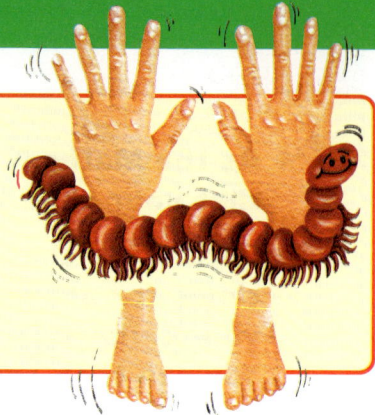

> When you multiply a number by 10, the decimal point appears to move one place to the right. Make sure that you understand why. For example, 3.2 means 3 units and 2 tenths of a unit. Multiplied by ten this becomes 3 tens and 2 units.

1 Multiply these numbers by 10. The first one in each group has been done for you.

a) i) $5 \times 10 = 50$ ii) 97 iii) 252 iv) 1103 v) 13465

b) i) $3.2 \times 10 = 32$ ii) 6.8 iii) 11.4 iv) 15.6 v) 126.8

c) i) $6.85 \times 10 = 68.5$ ii) 7.52 iii) 12.24 iv) 14.63 v) 121.64

2 Write the missing numbers.

a) $58 \times 10 = $ ◆?

b) ◆? $\times 10 = 38.2$

c) $148 \times $ ◆? $= 1480$

d) $1.44 \times 10 = $ ◆?

e) ◆? $\times 10 = 2240$

f) ◆? $\times 10 = 24.2$

> When you multiply a number by 100, the decimal point appears to move two places to the right. Make sure that you understand why. For example 4.85 means 4 units, 8 tenths and 5 hundredths of a unit. Multiplied by 100 this becomes 4 hundreds, 8 tens and 5 units.

3 Now multiply these numbers by 100. The first one in each set has been done for you.

a) (i) $2 \times 100 = 200$
   (ii) 38 (iii) 94 (iv) 218 (v) 346

b) (i) $4.85 \times 100 = 485$
   (ii) 16.54 (iii) 14.02 (iv) 113.04 (v) 1100.02

c) (i) $27.358 \times 100 = 2735.8$
   (ii) 28.002 (iii) 340.013 (iv) 62.4 (v) 78.09

4 Copy and complete these.

a) ◆? $\times 100 = 6400$

b) ◆? $\times 100 = 41\,100$

c) $100 \times $ ◆? $= 148\,100$

d) ◆? $\times 100 = 615.98$

5 Try multiplying these larger numbers.

a) 38.4×1000

b) 46.083×1000

c) $147.23 \times 10\,000$

d) $234.06 \times 10\,000$

e) $4.3474 \times 10\,000$

f) $0.242 \times 10\,000$

4

6 Divide these numbers by 10. The first two have been done for you.

a) $31 \div 10 = 3.1$ c) 180 e) 13.74 g) 232.4 i) 1.135

b) $4.6 \div 10 = 0.46$ d) 13.8 f) 10.37 h) 2.604

7 Complete these divisions.

a) $246 \div 100 = $ **?** f) $2358 \div 100 = $ **?**

b) $1246 \div $ **?** $ = 12.46$ g) **?** $ \div 10 = 6421$

c) $140 \div 10 = $ **?** h) $26\,345 \div $ **?** $ = 263.45$

d) **?** $ \div 100 = 3.485$ i) **?** $ \div 100 = 0.35$

e) **?** $ \div 10 = 25$

8 Solve these problems.

a) Harry has eight packs of jelly beans and there are 100 beans in each pack. How many jelly beans has he got?

b) George has 150 sweets and he wishes to divide them equally among his ten friends. How many will he give each friend?

c) I build a wall using 100 bricks per row. The total length of a row is 2480 cm. What is the length of each brick?

d) A car can travel 13.4 km for every litre of fuel used. How far will it travel on 100 litres?

e) I wish to make 100 skipping ropes each measuring 2.25 metres. How much rope will I need?

f) I can get exactly 1000 cupfuls of water from a tank holding 24 536 centilitres of water. How many centilitres does each cup hold?

g) If a lottery prize of £23 646 is won by a group of 100 people, how much does each winner get?

You could check your answers by multiplying them by 10.

Notice that what you are doing is the reverse of the work on the previous page.

Even though some of these questions deal with big numbers, they are easy if you think about what maths you need to use.

Test question

I can travel 334 602 metres on 100 litres of fuel.

How many metres can I travel on **1 litre**?

There are 1000 metres in a kilometre.

How many **kilometres per litre** can I drive?

Answers and Guidance are given on p.37.

How long did you take?

2 Probability

What's it all about?

★ In this chapter you will be comparing probabilities of spinners, using fractions in your answers. **Write your answers on a separate sheet of paper, showing your working.**

★ In your Maths National Test you may be asked to explain the probability of a particular number occurring on a spinner.

> Look back at Book 1 if you need to remind yourself about some of the words used to describe probability.

1 Look at this spinner.

How many sections are there on it?

Each section is $\frac{1}{6}$ of the whole spinner.

> Each section is $\frac{1}{8}$ of the spinner. So three sections is $\frac{3}{8}$ of the spinner.

2 How many sections are there on this spinner?

Answer these questions. Write your answers as fractions.

a) One section is  of the whole spinner.

b) Two sections are 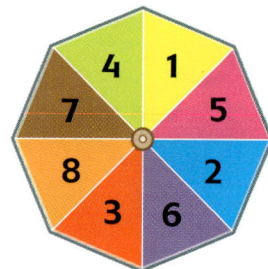 of the whole spinner.

c) Three sections are 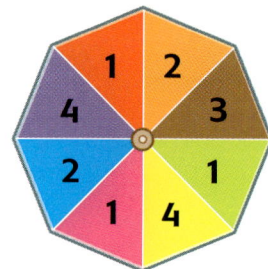 of the whole spinner.

3 Look at this spinner, then answer the questions.

Give your answers as fractions.

Explain each of your answers.

The first one has been done for you.

What is the probability of scoring:

> If there is no chance of an event happening you write 0. You must write a number. You will not get marks if you write a description, such as 'impossible'.

a) 1

Answer: $\frac{3}{8}$

Reason: There are eight equal sections on the spinner, so there are eight different ways of the spinner landing – three of these ways score 1.

b) 5

c) 3

d) either a 2 or a 4

e) an odd number?

> If you have difficulty with this, look back at Book 2, Chapter 11.

4 Compare these fractions. Write down whether the second fraction is larger, smaller or the same as the first.

a) $\frac{4}{8}$ or $\frac{2}{4}$ c) $\frac{2}{4}$ or $\frac{3}{8}$ e) $\frac{2}{6}$ or $\frac{1}{3}$

b) $\frac{1}{3}$ or $\frac{3}{6}$ d) $\frac{3}{6}$ or $\frac{3}{4}$ f) $\frac{4}{6}$ or $\frac{1}{4}$

When you answer questions comparing probabilities, you need to give a mathematical explanation (one using numbers).

5 Look at these two spinners, then answer the questions. Give a reason for your answer in each case.

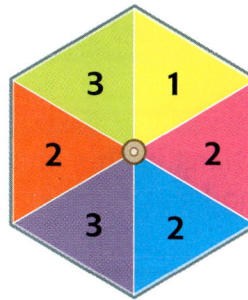

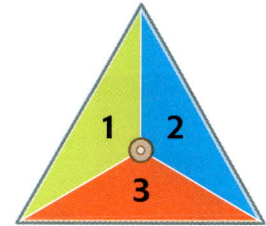

Spinner A   Spinner B

a) What is the probability of spinning a 3 on spinner A? Write your answer as a fraction.

b) Is there the same probability of spinning a 3 on spinner A as on spinner B?

c) On which spinner are you more likely to spin a 2?

d) On which spinner are you more likely to spin a 1?

Remember a probability of $\frac{1}{4}$ is the same as probability of $\frac{2}{8}$.

6 Draw a spinner with eight equal sections. Give your spinner a probability of:

a) $\frac{1}{4}$ of spinning a 2

b) $\frac{1}{8}$ of spinning a 6

c) $\frac{3}{8}$ of spinning a 4

d) $\frac{1}{4}$ of spinning an 8.

Test question

Here are two spinners.

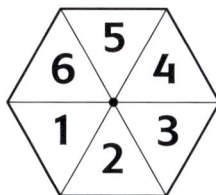

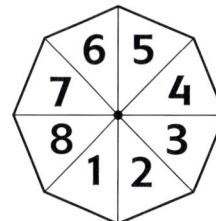

Jill's spinner   **Peter's spinner**

Jill says, 'I am more likely than Peter to spin a 3.'

Give a reason why she is correct.

Jill is correct because …

Peter says, 'We are both equally likely to spin an even number.'

Give a reason why he is correct.

Peter is correct because …

Answers and Guidance are given on pp.37–38.

How long did you take?

3 Multiplying larger numbers

What's it all about?

★ The questions in this chapter give you practice in multiplying large numbers.

★ They break down the sums into a series of steps to remind you of what you are really doing when you do a long multiplication sum.

★ You may be asked to use long multiplication to solve everyday problems in your Maths National Test.

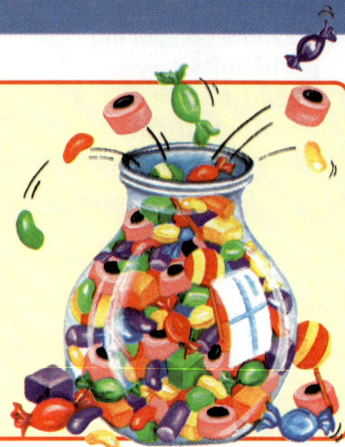

1 Write what these numbers mean. The first two have been done for you.

a) 421 = 4 hundreds, 2 tens, 1 unit

b) 629 = 6 hundreds, 2 tens, 9 units

c) 972 = **?** hundreds, **?** tens, **?** units

d) 452 = **?**

e) 895 = **?**

f) 674 = **?**

g) 750 = **?**

h) 503 = **?**

When you multiply the first time you are multiplying units. When you multiply the second time you are multiplying tens. When you are sure that you understand this, you can do them as a single sum,

e.g.
```
   23
  × 6
  138
   1
```

2 Multiply these larger numbers using the method shown in a) and b). Then do them again using the method shown in the margin note.

a)
```
              23
             × 6
  6 × 3       18
  6 × 20     120
             138
```

b)
```
              29
             × 4
  4 × 9       36
  4 × 20      80
             116
```

c)
```
    68
   × 7
```

d)
```
    82
   × 8
```

e)
```
    76
   × 9
```

f)
```
    36
   × 5
```

g)
```
    71
   × 8
```

h)
```
    89
   × 6
```

3 Try these even larger numbers. Use either of the two methods shown.

a)
```
                465
               × 4
  4 × 5          20     (multiplying the units)
  4 × 60        240     (multiplying the tens)
  4 × 400      1600     (multiplying the hundreds)
              1860
```

b)
```
     479
    × 7
   3353
    5 6
```

Remember to carry numbers correctly, from units to tens and from tens to hundreds.

c)
```
   134
  × 7
```

d)
```
   576
  × 8
```

e)
```
   409
  × 9
```

f)
```
   327
  × 5
```

g)
```
   786
  × 8
```

h)
```
   972
  × 6
```

To multiply by 20, you multiply by 10 and then by 2. So 26 × 20 = 260 × 2 = 520. If you understand this, you won't forget the zero.

This is just one way of doing long multiplication. There are lots of others.

4 Try multiplying a two-digit number by another two-digit number. The first two have been done for you.

a)
```
              29
            × 27
  7 × 29     203
 20 × 29     580
             783
```

c)
```
     53
   × 37
   ____
```

e)
```
     69
   × 39
   ____
```

g)
```
     71
   × 48
   ____
```

b)
```
              76
            × 48
  8 × 76     608
 40 × 76    3040
            3648
```

d)
```
     97
   × 84
   ____
```

f)
```
     85
   × 56
   ____
```

h)
```
     99
   × 62
   ____
```

5 Now try multiplying a three-digit number by a two-digit number.

a)
```
               436
             × 21
  1 × 436      436
 20 × 436     8720
              9156
                 1
```

c)
```
    158
  × 35
  ____
```

e)
```
    389
  × 46
  ____
```

g)
```
    973
  × 78
  ____
```

b)
```
               876
             × 78
  8 × 876     7008
 70 × 876    61320
             68328
```

d)
```
    267
  × 24
  ____
```

f)
```
    491
  × 89
  ____
```

h)
```
    809
  × 63
  ____
```

6 Solve these multiplication problems.

a) If there are 144 bags of sweets in a box and a shop has 26 boxes delivered, how many bags are there altogether?

b) 76 coaches seating 52 supporters arrive for a match. How many supporters does this make?

c) A farm produces 846 trays of eggs containing 24 eggs. What is the total number of eggs?

Test question

Show your working. You may get a mark.

Calculate 431 × 23.

Answers and Guidance are given on pp.38–39.

How long did you take?

4 Nets

What's it all about?

★ In this chapter you will draw and construct three-dimensional (3D) shapes using nets.

★ Your Maths National Test may ask you to identify or draw a net for a given shape.

> You will need scissors, paper or thin card, a ruler, a pencil, and a protractor for this page.

> A 3D shape has depth as well as height and width. You can hold a 3D shape.

1 Find a cardboard cuboid. Any empty box, such as a cereal packet, will do.

Cut open the top and bottom, then cut down a vertical fold.
Open out your shape.

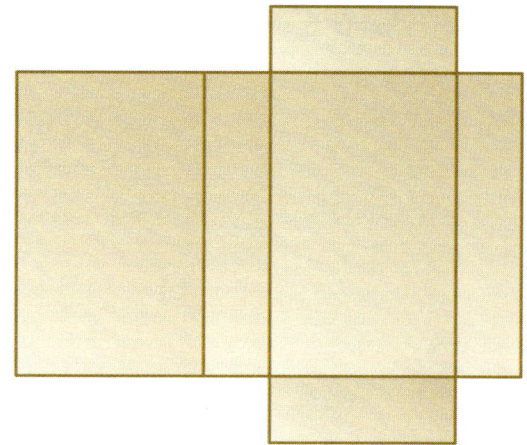

You now have a net of a cuboid.

> A **face** is a side and **vertices** are corners.

2 Think about a cube.

a) What shape are its faces?

b) How many faces does it have?

c) How many vertices does it have?

d) How many edges does it have?

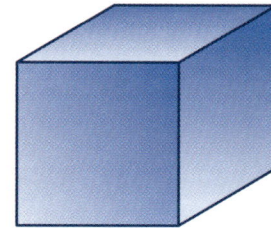

3 Cut out six squares.

Arrange them into this shape.

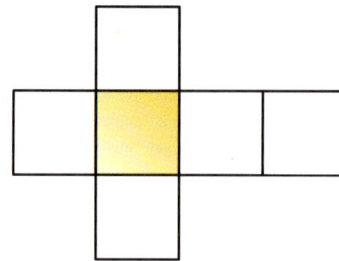

> It does not matter what size the squares are, but they must all be the **same** size.

Draw round the outside of this shape and then cut it out.

Fold it into a 3D shape.

a) What 3D shape have you made?

b) Try different ways of placing the six squares with at least one edge touching another square. Try to make each into a cube.

Are all your arrangements nets of cubes?

4 Look at this square-based pyramid.

  a) There are two different shapes of faces. What are they?

  b) How many faces does a square-based pyramid have?

  c) Using squared paper, draw this shape as accurately as you can.

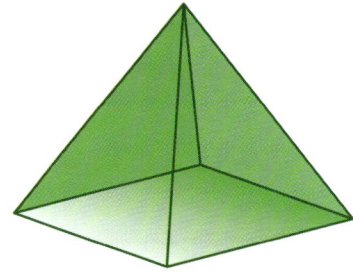

You will need to measure carefully. The triangles must all be the same size.

Make your folds really sharp. This will help you to make accurate 3D shapes.

The angles of the triangle should each be 60°.

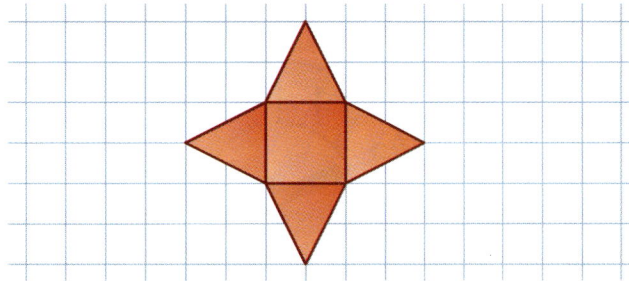

  d) Cut out your shape and fold it into the 3D shape.

5 Draw this shape onto thin card or paper.

Cut it out and fold it. What shape can you make from this net?

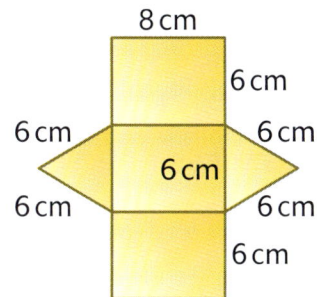

8 cm
6 cm
6 cm
6 cm
6 cm
6 cm
6 cm
6 cm

Test question

This is an open top box.

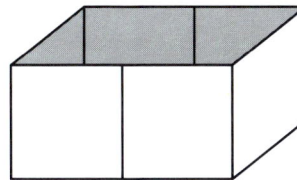

Put a tick (✓) for each diagram **if it is a net** for the box.

Put a cross (✗) if it is not.

The base is shaded in each one.

A   B   C   D

Answers and Guidance are given on p.39.

How long did you take?

11

You should be able to complete these questions in 10 minutes

1 Write in the missing **three-digit** number.

$$\boxed{}\boxed{}\boxed{} \div 10 = 20$$

1 mark

2 Lee has two spinners.

 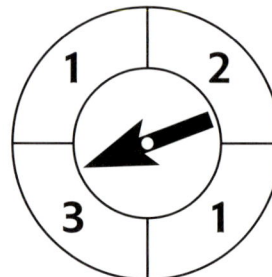

A   B

What is the probability of spinning a **4** on **spinner A**?

Write your answer as a fraction.

1 mark

On which spinner is he **more likely** to get a **1**?

Give a reason for your answer.

1 mark

3

Fares to France

Adults	£23
Children	£11.50

There are **2 adults** and **3 children** in a family.

How much does it cost the **family** to go on the ferry?

1 mark

4   Here is a triangular box.

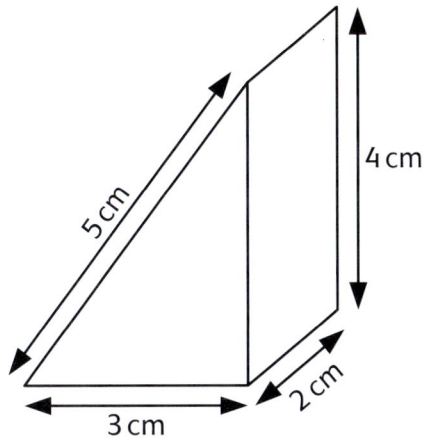

Below is part of the net of the box, but **two** of its faces are missing.

Draw **accurately**, full size, **one** of the missing faces on the diagram below.

You can use a ruler and protractor (angle measurer).

2 marks

5 Negative numbers

> Remember that the largest negative number will begin the ordering.

1 Put these numbers into order of size. The first is in the correct order.

a)	−50	−12	−6	2	11	42
b)	−8	−11	3	9	−9	−35	−2
c)	−4	4	6	9	2	−3	−1
d)	−9	8	6	3	0	−2	−1
e)	100	−89	111	−58	98	−94	0

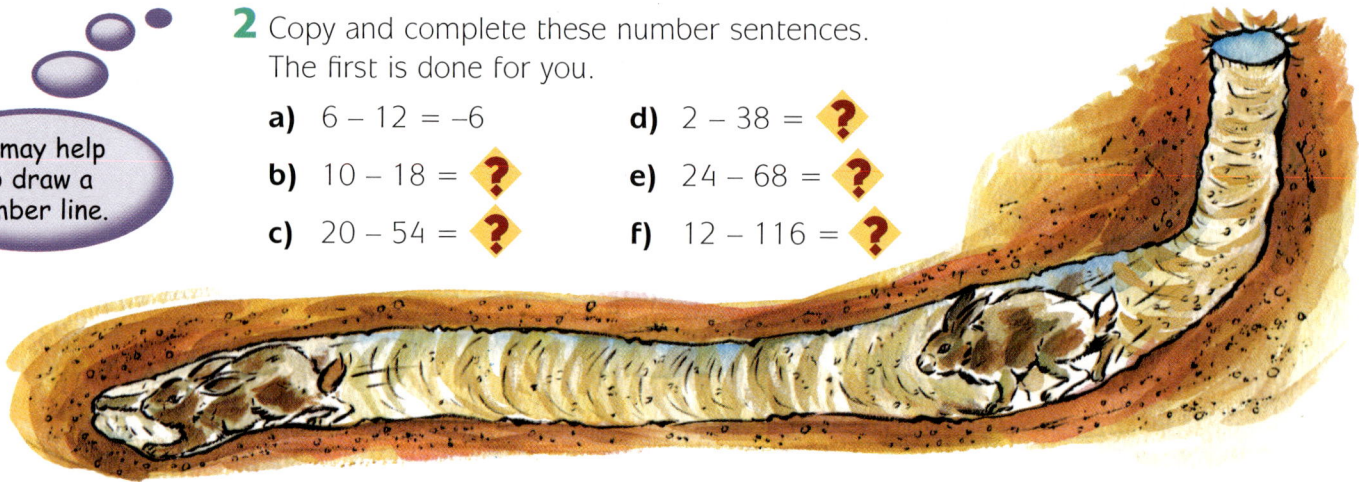

> It may help to draw a number line.

2 Copy and complete these number sentences. The first is done for you.

a) $6 - 12 = -6$ **d)** $2 - 38 = $?

b) $10 - 18 = $?   **e)** $24 - 68 = $?

c) $20 - 54 = $?   **f)** $12 - 116 = $?

> We do not put '+' in front of a positive number unless there is a specific reason, for instance to make some data extra clear.

3 Complete these sequences. The rule is given in each case. The first one is done for you.

a)	**Rule:** subtract 3	9	6	3	0	−3	−6		
b)	**Rule:** subtract 6	18	?	6	0	?	?	−18	
c)	**Rule:** subtract 5	15	10	?	?	?	−10	?	?
d)	**Rule:** subtract 9	22	13	?	−5	?	?	−32	
e)	**Rule:** subtract 4	11	7	?	?	?	−9	?	?

> Notice you can have different scales on the vertical and horizontal axes.

4 Write the numbers on the axes on these grids. The first has been done for you.

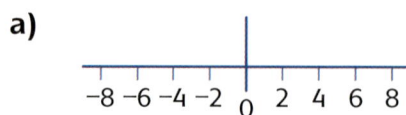

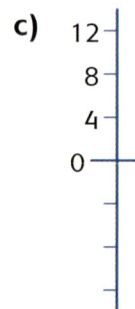

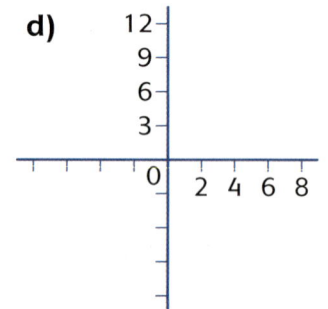

a)

−8 −6 −4 −2 0 2 4 6 8

b)

0 3 6 9

c)

12
8
4
0

d)

12
9
6
3
0 2 4 6 8

5 Solve these problems.

a) On 22 December the daytime temperature in Chicago was 3°C. On 23 December it was −10°C. By how many degrees had the temperature dropped?

b) During a freezing night in winter the temperature dropped from −1°C to −8°C. By how many degrees had the temperature dropped?

c) A miner goes down into a mine to a depth of −40 metres. He goes up 5 metres and then down a further 15 metres. How far below the surface is he now?

d) A pot-holer descends into a cave to a depth of −100 metres and, after exploring goes up to a depth of −68 metres. How far has he ascended (gone up)?

6 John has set himself a target of 60 metres for throwing a cricket ball. He records his attempts to the nearest metre above and below his target.

+10   −16   +12   −10   −3   +2

Remember −3 means 3 m less than his target. You might want to write out a chart with the actual lengths thrown written on it.

a) How long was his best throw?

b) How long was his shortest throw?

c) What was the length of the throw which was nearest to his target of 60 metres?

7 The newsagent wants to sell 100 papers every day. He records his sales for a week, writing down how many more or less than his target he sells.

Sun	Mon	Tues	Wed	Thurs	Fri	Sat
+5	+25	−16	−4	+8	−2	+32

Remember −4 means 4 less than the target of 100 papers. You might want to write out a chart with the actual sales figures written on it.

a) What was his best selling day? How many papers did he sell?

b) What was his worst day? How many papers did he sell?

c) What was the difference between his sales on Wednesday and on Monday?

d) His target for the whole week was 700. By how many papers did he miss or go over his target?

Test question

Here is a table of temperatures at dawn on the same day.

What is the **difference** in temperature between **London** and **Paris**? [ ] °C

At noon the temperature in **New York** has risen by 5°C.

What is the temperature in **New York** at noon? [ ] °C

	Temperatures °C
London	−4°
Moscow	−6°
New York	−9°
Paris	+6°
Sydney	+14°

Answers and Guidance are given on pp.39–40.

How long did you take?

6 Fractions

What's it all about?

★ These pages remind you how to find fractions of whole numbers.

★ In your Maths National Test you may be asked to use fractions to solve problems.

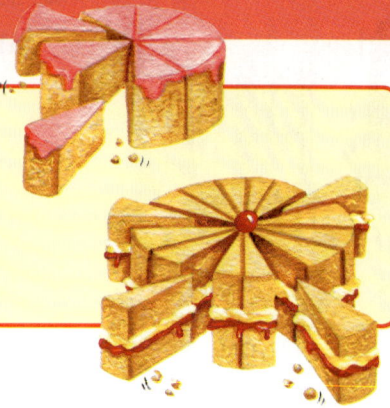

> Continue to use counters to help you for as long as you think you need them.

1 Count out 15 counters. Divide them into five groups. How many are there in each group?

Complete: $\frac{1}{5}$ of 15 = ◆❓

2 Find these amounts. The first two have been done for you.

a) $\frac{1}{3}$ of 18 = 18 ÷ 3 = 6

b) $\frac{1}{4}$ of 4 = 4 ÷ 4 = 1

c) $\frac{1}{3}$ of 6

d) $\frac{1}{5}$ of 20

e) $\frac{1}{6}$ of 12

f) $\frac{1}{8}$ of 24

g) $\frac{1}{10}$ of 10

h) $\frac{1}{9}$ of 18

> You find the answer by dividing the number by the denominator of the fraction.

5 numerator

6 denominator

3 Work out these amounts. Use a calculator if you need to.

a) $\frac{1}{6}$ of 84

b) $\frac{1}{9}$ of 135

c) $\frac{1}{7}$ of 112

d) $\frac{1}{4}$ of 104

e) $\frac{1}{5}$ of 115

f) $\frac{1}{3}$ of 51

g) $\frac{1}{2}$ of 66

h) $\frac{1}{8}$ of 168

> Knowing your tables will help you to complete these sums.

4 Find these amounts. The first two have been done for you.

a) $\frac{2}{3}$ of 72 $\frac{1}{3}$ of 72 = 24 so $\frac{2}{3}$ of 72 = 2 × 24 = 48

b) $\frac{4}{6}$ of 36 $\frac{1}{6}$ of 36 = 6 so $\frac{4}{6}$ of 36 = 4 × 6 = 24

c) $\frac{2}{8}$ of 56

d) $\frac{3}{5}$ of 75

e) $\frac{4}{9}$ of 63

f) $\frac{3}{4}$ × 80

g) $\frac{2}{6}$ × 108

h) $\frac{6}{10}$ × 130

> The word 'of' can be replaced with a × sign, so $\frac{1}{3}$ of 15 is usually written $\frac{1}{3}$ × 15.

When you reduce fractions to their simplest form, always divide the top (the numerator) and the bottom (the denominator) by the same amount. If you need more help, see Book 2, Chapter 11.

5 Reduce these fractions to their simplest form. The first two have been done for you.

a) $\frac{16}{20} = \frac{8}{10} = \frac{4}{5}$

b) $\frac{18}{36} = \frac{9}{18} = \frac{3}{6}$

c) $\frac{16}{32}$

d) $\frac{60}{100}$

e) $\frac{30}{50}$

f) $\frac{12}{42}$

g) $\frac{36}{48}$

h) $\frac{36}{72}$

i) $\frac{50}{100}$

j) $\frac{28}{35}$

6 Work out these fractions, reduce them to their simplest form. The first two are done for you.

a) 5 is $\frac{5}{20}$ of 20 $\frac{5}{20} = \frac{1}{4}$

b) 8 is $\frac{8}{16}$ of 16 $\frac{8}{16} = \frac{1}{2}$

c) 12 is ? of 36 $\frac{12}{36}$ = ?

d) 2 is ? of 18 $\frac{2}{18}$ = ?

e) 16 is ? of 24   ? = ?

f) 20 is ? of 30   ? = ?

g) 35 is ? of 50   ? = ?

h) 27 is ? of 36   ? = ?

7 Solve these problems. Show your working. The first one is done for you.

a) If there are 15 children and 10 go to the seaside. What fraction of the children go?

Working: $\frac{10}{15} = \frac{2}{5}$

Answer: $\frac{2}{5}$ go to the seaside.

b) There are 35 children in a class but $\frac{1}{5}$ are away with flu. How many are away?

c) Sam has 40 sweets. He gives $\frac{1}{4}$ to his friend. How many sweets does he give her?

d) A class borrowed 28 library books. 21 books are returned. What fraction of the books are returned?

e) In a bowl of 21 pieces of fruit, $\frac{1}{7}$ are bananas. How many bananas are there?

Test question

Linda has 30 marbles and five are blue.

What **fraction** of her marbles are **blue**?

She says that $\frac{2}{5}$ of her marbles are red.

How many **red marbles** does she have?

Answers and Guidance are given on pp.40–41.

How long did you take?

7 Missing numbers

What's it all about?

★ The questions in this chapter will remind you how multiplication and division are related.

★ In your Maths National Test, you may be asked to find a missing number by using multiplication and division.

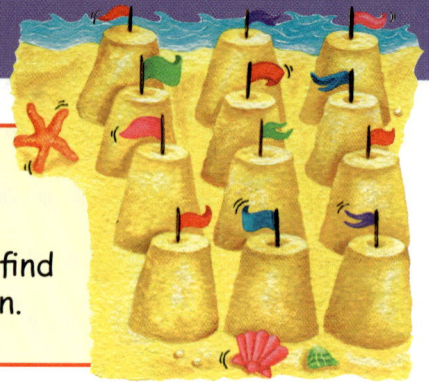

You will need to use either your 3 times table or your 7 times table here.

1 Find 21 objects (anything will do). Divide them into seven groups. How many in each group?

a) $21 \div 7 = $?

Put them together again.

b) $7 \times 3 = $?

Now divide them into three groups. How many in each group?

c) $21 \div 3 = $?

d) $3 \times 7 = $?

2 Take 18 objects. Divide them into three groups.

a) $18 \div 3 = $?

Put them together again.

b) $6 \times 3 = $?

Now divide them into six groups. How many in each group?

c) $18 \div 6 = $?   d) $3 \times 6 = $?

3 Using the same 18 objects, repeat the task. This time divide them into nine groups. and then into two groups. Complete these four sums.

a) $18 \div 9 = $?   c) $18 \div $? $ = $?

b) $9 \times $? $ = $?   d) ? $ \times $? $ = $?

4 Write four similar sums for each of these numbers. The first one is done for you.

6 and 12 are factors of 72 (see Book 1, Chapter 5 and Book 2, Chapter 2).

a) 72   b) 10   c) 56   d) 27   e) 45   f) 42
$72 \div 6 = 12$
$72 \div 12 = 6$
$6 \times 12 = 72$
$12 \times 6 = 72$

You should not need to do any calculations! Use what you have learned from the previous questions.

5 Now try these.

a) $276 \times 35 = 9660$ b) $31 \times 42 = 1302$ c) $26 \times 91 = $?

$35 \times 276 = $? $42 \times 31 = $? $91 \times 26 = $?

$9660 \div 35 = $? $1302 \div 31 = $? $2366 \div 91 = $?

$9660 \div 276 = $? $1302 \div 42 = $? $2366 \div 26 = $?

You may need a calculator for the first sum in each group. After that, you should be able to work out the others by using what you have learned about how division and multiplication are related.

6 Now try these.

a)
$379 \times 27 =$ ❓
$27 \times 379 =$ ❓
$10\,233 \div 27 =$ ❓
$10\,233 \div 379 =$ ❓

b)
$163 \times 59 =$ ❓
$59 \times 163 =$ ❓
$9617 \div 59 =$ ❓
❓ $\div 163 =$ ❓

c)
$228 \times 91 =$ ❓
$91 \times 228 =$ ❓
$20\,748 \div 91 =$ ❓
$20\,748 \div$ ❓ $=$ ❓

7 Complete these groups.

a)
$33 \times 356 =$ ❓
❓ $\times 33 =$ ❓
❓ $\div 33 =$ ❓
$11\,748 \div$ ❓ $=$ ❓

b)
$24 \times 192 =$ ❓
❓ $\times 24 =$ ❓
❓ $\div 24 =$ ❓
❓ $\div 192 =$ ❓

c)
$42 \times 220 =$ ❓
❓ $\times$ ❓ $=$ ❓
❓ $\div$ ❓ $=$ ❓
❓ $\div$ ❓ $=$ ❓

d)
$267 \times 28 =$ ❓
❓ $\times$ ❓ $=$ ❓
❓ $\div$ ❓ $=$ ❓
❓ $\div$ ❓ $=$ ❓

e)
$9212 \div 14 =$ ❓
❓ $\div$ ❓ $=$ ❓
❓ $\times$ ❓ $=$ ❓
❓ $\times$ ❓ $=$ ❓

f)
$14\,364 \div 19 =$ ❓
❓ $\div$ ❓ $=$ ❓
❓ $\times$ ❓ $=$ ❓
❓ $\times$ ❓ $=$ ❓

If you have trouble with these, try writing the whole group as you did in question 7.

8 Write down the sum you would do to work out the following. The first has been done for you.

a) $23 \times$ ❓ $= 1288$

Working: $1288 \div 23 = 56$
Answer: $23 \times \mathbf{56} = 1288$

b) ❓ $\times 34 = 3026$

c) $1352 \div$ ❓ $= 26$

d) $1065 \div$ ❓ $= 71$

9 Now solve these.

a) $21\,845 \div$ ❓ $= 85$

b) $16\,029 \div$ ❓ $= 411$

c) $51\,142 \div$ ❓ $= 91$

d) $8924 \div$ ❓ $= 194$

You could check your answers by multiplying the answer by the number you divided by.

Test question

Write the **missing** number.

$10\,233 \div \boxed{} = 379$

Answers and Guidance are given on pp.41–42

How long did you take?

8 Area and perimeter

> In metric units, area is measured in square centimetres (cm^2), square metres (m^2), square kilometres (km^2)...

1 Calculate the area of each of these shapes. They have all been drawn with centimetre squares.

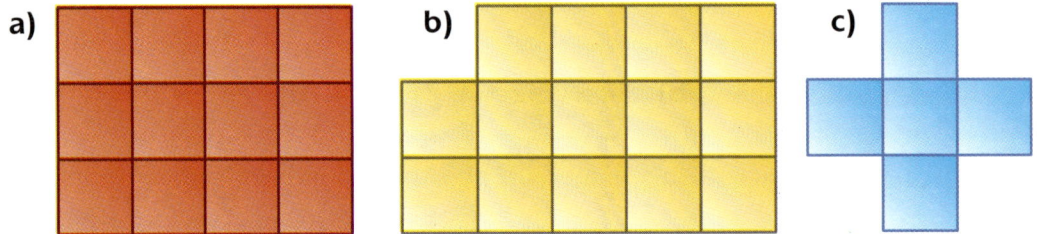

a)

b)

c)

> To calculate the area of a rectangle you need to multiply the base measurement by the height measurement. If you are not sure why, look at shape (a) in question 1. It has three rows with four centimetre squares in each row: $4 \times 3 = 12$.

2 Calculate the areas of these rectangles. The first has been done for you.

a) Area = $13 \times 7 = 91\,m^2$
13 cm
7 cm

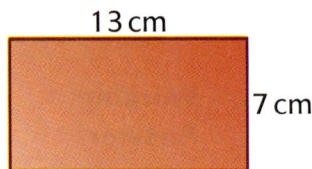

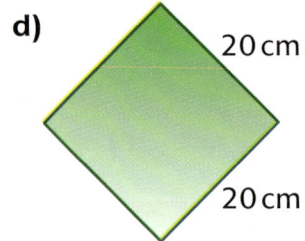

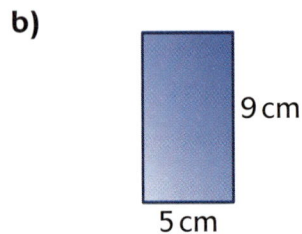

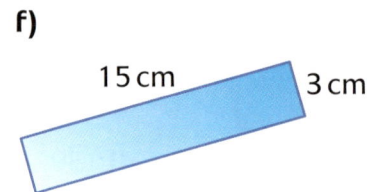

b)
9 cm
5 cm

c)
12 cm
4 cm

d)
20 cm
20 cm

e)
16 cm
2 cm

f)
15 cm
3 cm

> Remember that the perimeter is the distance around the outside edge of a shape.

3 Calculate the perimeter of each of these shapes. Shape (c) is a square.

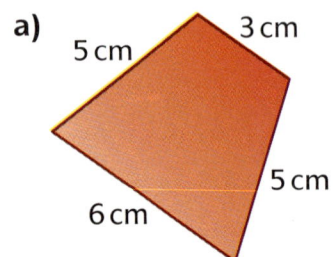

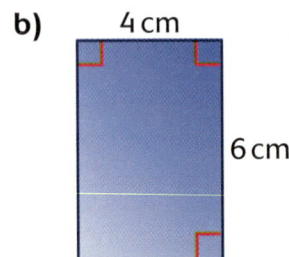

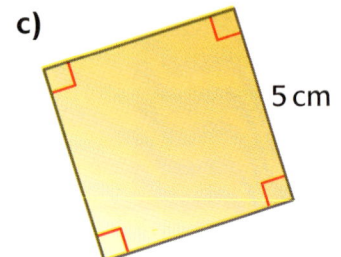

a)
5 cm
3 cm
5 cm
6 cm

b)
4 cm
6 cm

c)
5 cm

Why were you only given one measurement for shape (c)?

Sometimes you can pair up half rectangles to make the calculation easier.

4 These shapes are drawn with centimetre squares. Work out their areas. The first has been done for you.

a)

Area = 5 whole squares and 3 half squares
= $6\frac{1}{2}$ cm^2

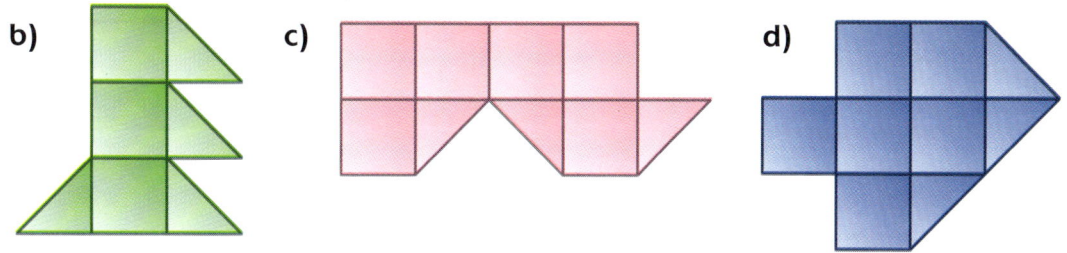

b)

c)

d)

The diagonal of a rectangle divides it into two halves. To find the area of half a rectangle, calculate the area of the whole rectangle and then divide by two!

5 Calculate the areas of the shaded parts in these rectangles – each is half the rectangle. The first one has been done for you.

a)

3 cm
6 cm

Area of the triangle = $\frac{1}{2} \times 3 \times 6 = 18 \div 2$
= 9 cm^2

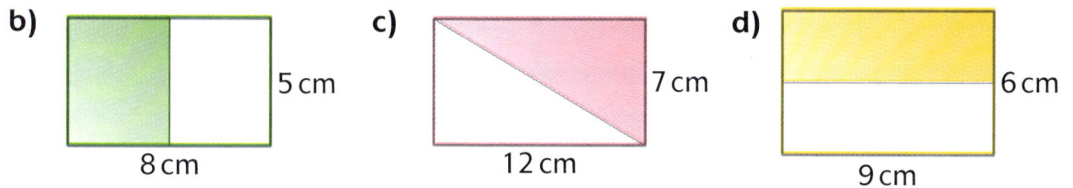

b)

5 cm
8 cm

c)

7 cm
12 cm

d)

6 cm
9 cm

A half rectangle may be a triangle or another rectangle.

6 Calculate the areas of these shapes. Each square has sides of 5 cm.

a)

b)

c)

d)

Test question

This plan of a garden is made of rectangles and triangles.

The area of each **rectangle** is **12 square metres**.

What is the **area** of the **whole garden**?

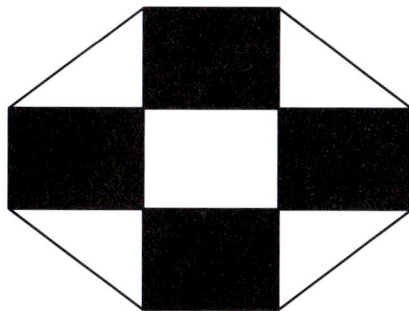

Answers and Guidance are given on p.42.

How long did you take?

National Test Questions 2

You should be able to complete these questions in 14 minutes

1 Circle two numbers with a difference of 8.

–5 –4 –3 –2 –1 0 1 2 3 4 5

1 mark

2 There are three classes in Tregarth Primary School.

On one day in November, a lot of children are ill.

Complete this grid.

Class	Number of children in the class	Fraction of the children away	Number of children away
1		$\frac{2}{11}$	6
2	30	$\frac{3}{10}$	
3	35		14

1 mark
1 mark
1 mark

3 Complete this.

$\square \div 15 = 32$

1 mark

4 On the grid below, draw a **square** with an **area** of **2 cm²**.

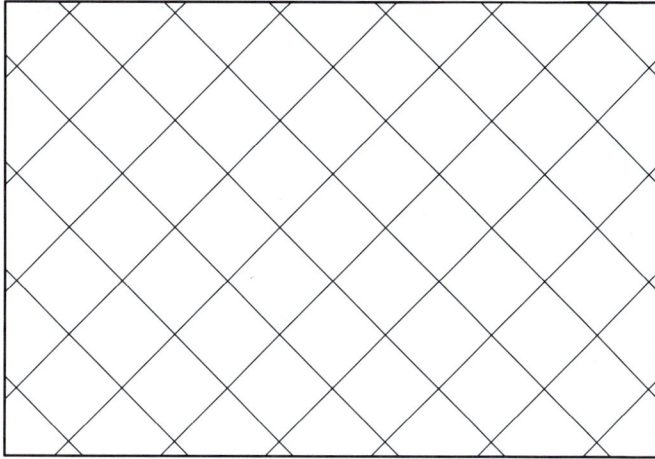

1 mark

5   Dice 1   Dice 2

   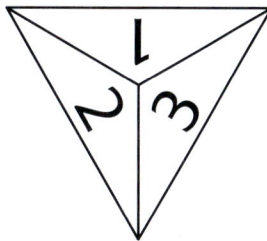

Dice 1 has six sides numbered 1, 2, 3, 4, 5, 6.

Dice 2 has four sides numbered 1, 2, 3, 4.

If I throw **both dice together**, what is the probability that I will throw a **1**?

1 mark

If I throw **both dice together**, what is the probability that I will score a **total of 11**?

1 mark

9 Conversion of units

What's it all about?

★ In this chapter you will revise conversion of metric units.

★ You will also revise how imperial units relate to metric ones.

> milli – thousandth
> centi – hundredth
> kilo – thousand.
> So 1 millimetre is $\frac{1}{1000}$ of a metre and 1 kilometre is 1000 metres.

1 Copy and complete the conversion table for these measurements of **length**.

1 metre (m) = **?** centimetres (cm)	
1 metre = **?** millimetres (mm)	
1 kilometre = **?** metres	

2 Use your table to work these out.

1 kilometre = **?** centimetres   1 metre = **?** millimetres

1 kilometre = **?** millimetres   1 centimetre = **?** millimetres

> If you need help in multiplying 10s, 100s or 1000s, look back to Chapter 1.

3 Write conversions for these measures of **mass** and **capacity**.

Mass	Capacity	
1000 grams (g) = **?** kilogram (kg)	1 litre (l) = **?** centilitres (cl)	
	1 litre = **?** millilitres (ml)	
	1 centilitre (cl) = **?** millilitres	

4 Which metric unit of measurement would you use to measure:

a) the length of a room   e) the length of an insect

b) the distance to Paris   f) the size of an exercise book

c) the amount of flour for a cake   g) cola in a can

d) your weight   h) water for making pastry?
                                     Note: you need very little!

5 Write the equivalent amounts for each of these measurements. The first one has been done for you.

> Use the answers to questions 1, 2 and 3 to help you.

a) 1.75 m = 175 cm	d) 27.92 l = **?** cl	g) 15.64 cm = **?** mm
b) 2.46 kg = **?** g	e) 135 m = **?** cm	h) 87.6 cl = **?** ml
c) £4.28 = **?** pence	f) 9.5 km = **?** m	i) 4.78 l = **?** ml

> Think carefully about where you need to put the decimal point. If you need help, look back at Chapter 1.

6 Write the equivalent amounts for each of these measurements. The first has been done for you.

a) 93p = £0.93	d) 1476 g = **?** kg	g) 2423 m = **?** km
b) 325 cm = **?** m	e) 3116 ml = **?** l	h) 1212 mm = **?** cm
c) 264 cl = **?** l	f) 895 ml = **?** cl	i) 1714 ml = **?** l

7 Now try these. You need to think very carefully!

a) 671p = £ ?

b) 15.86 kg = ? g

c) £13.99 = ? pence

d) 9864 g = ? kg

e) 5935 ml = ? l

f) 659 ml = ? cl

g) 17.53 cm = ? mm

h) 75.8 cl = ? ml

i) 56.3 l = ? ml

You need to decide whether you are converting to bigger units (and so need to divide), or to smaller units (and need to multiply).

8 Write these measurement words onto pieces of paper. Mark on each whether it is a **metric** unit of measurement or an **imperial** one. Then sort them into four groups: mass, length, capacity, time.

gallon	metre	litre	century	pound	foot	minute
ounce	hour	inch	millilitre	yard	centimetre	
millennium	kilometre	millimetre	pint	decade	kilogram	
day	gram	year	mile	second		

Imperial measures:
12 inches (ins) = 1 foot (ft)
3 feet = 1 yard (yd)
36 inches = 1 yard
1 gallon = 8 pints (pts)
1 pound (lb) = 16 ounces (oz)

9 Copy these sentences, using only the correct word. The first has been done for you.

a) 1 litre is approximately 2 pints, so a litre is larger/~~smaller~~ than a pint.

b) 4.5 litres is approximately 1 gallon, so a litre is larger/smaller than a gallon.

c) 1 kilogram is approximately 2 pounds, so a kilogram is heavier/lighter than a pound.

d) 30 grams is approximately 1 oz, so a gram is heavier/lighter than an ounce.

e) 8 kilometres is approximately 5 miles, so a mile is longer/shorter than a kilometre.

f) 1 metre is approximately 39 inches, so a metre is longer/shorter than a yard.

g) 2.2 centimetres is approximately 1 inch, so a centimetre is longer/shorter than an inch.

You may need to ask an adult to help you with this.

10 Return to your groups of words from question 8, sort each group into order of size, starting with the biggest unit.

Test question

My car has a problem.

It uses 100 ml of oil every 50 kilometres.

If I put in **1 litre** of oil, **how far** can I drive safely?

Answers and Guidance are given on pp.42-43.

How long did you take?

10 Reflective symmetry

> You will need a sharp pencil and a ruler. Your drawings will need to be very accurate. Count the dots or squares carefully.

1 Reflect these shapes across the mirror line. The first has been done for you.

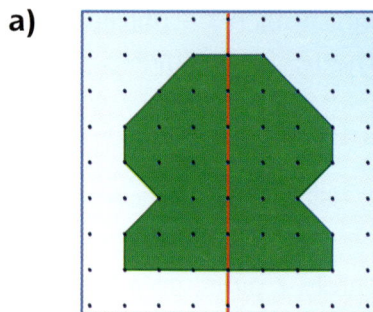

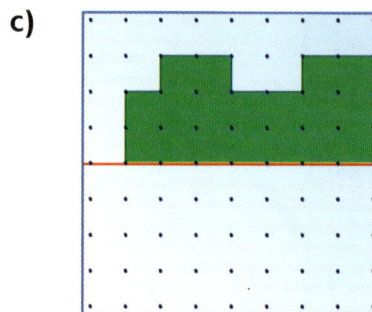

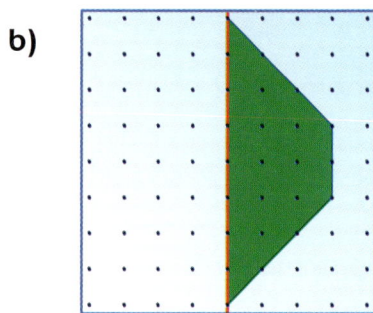

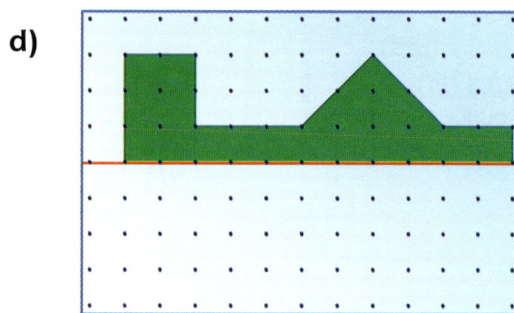

a)

c)

b)

d)

2 Reflect these shapes across the mirror line. In these reflections, the mirror line is not through the centre of the shape. The first one has been done for you.

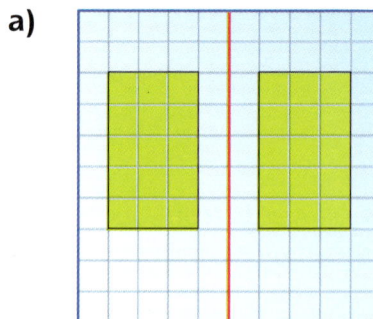

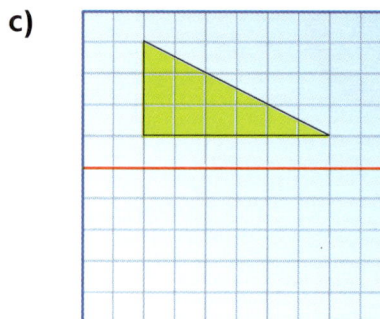

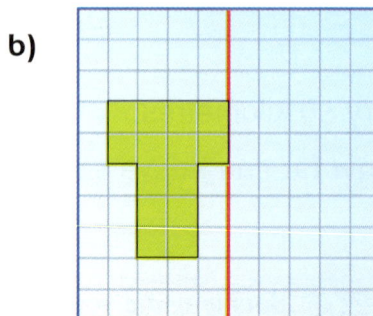

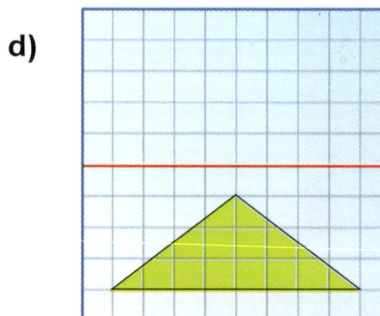

a)

c)

b)

d)

> Notice how the reflection is an exact copy of the shape across the mirror line and it is the same distance from the mirror line. Be careful to draw the shape the **right size** as well as in the **correct position**.

3 Complete these symmetrical patterns. The first one has been done for you.

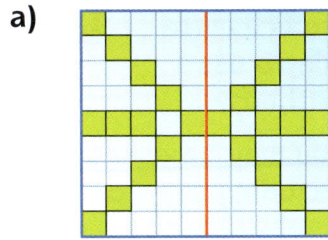

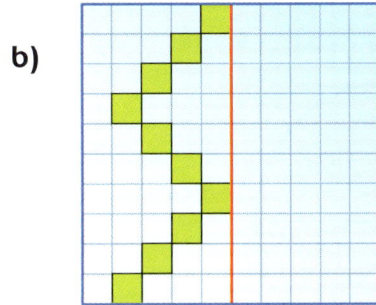

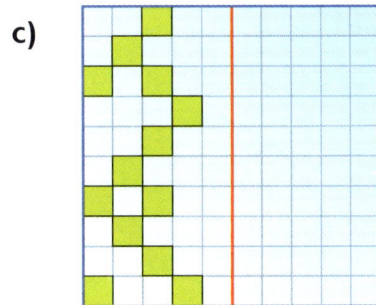

a)

b)

c)

4 Some symmetrical patterns have two lines of symmetry. Complete these patterns. The first has been done for you.

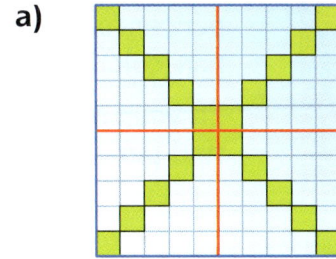

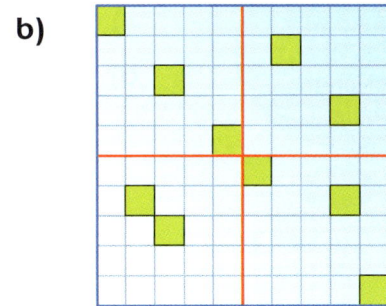

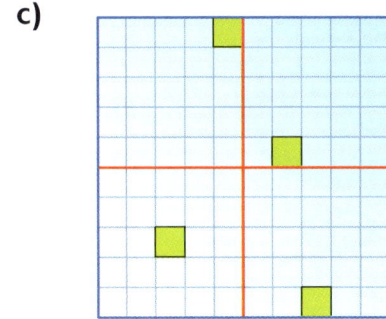

a)

b)

c)

Test question

Write the correct **letter** in this sentence.

Shape ☐ is **a reflection** of shape A.

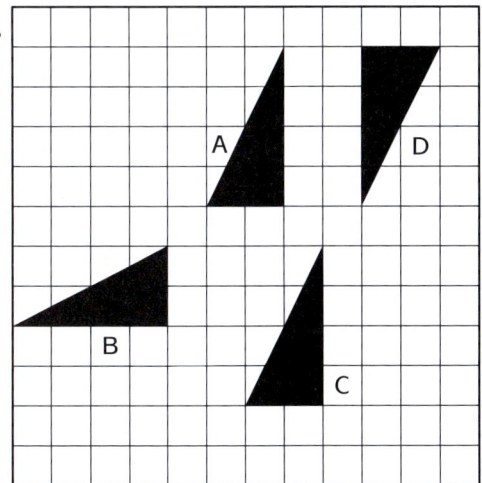

Answers and Guidance are given on pp.43–44.

How long did you take?

11 Percentages

What's it all about?

★ This chapter reminds you how to calculate percentages. You need to be able to use non-calculator and calculator methods.

★ In your Maths National Test, you may be asked to find percentages of numbers, including sums of money.

> A percentage is another way of talking about a fraction of a whole.

1 Using the diagram to help you, give these fractions as percentages.

a) $\frac{1}{2}$

b) $\frac{1}{4}$

c) $\frac{3}{4}$

d) 1

> To express a fraction as a decimal, divide the numerator by the denominator.

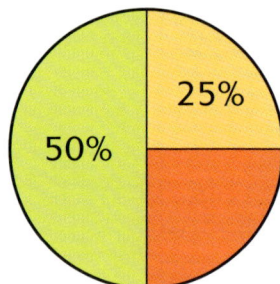

2 Using this diagram to help you, give these fractions first as decimals, then as percentages.

a) $\frac{1}{10} = 0.1 = $ ❓ %

b) $\frac{5}{10} = 0.5 = $ ❓ %

c) $\frac{3}{10} = $ ❓ $ = $ ❓ %

d) $\frac{7}{10} = $ ❓ $ = $ ❓ %

> 1% is $\frac{1}{100}$ of the whole, so to calculate 1% you need to divide the whole by 100.
>
> If you have difficulty with division by 100, look back at Chapter 1.

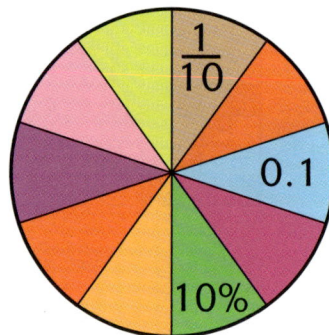

3 Calculate 1% of each of the following numbers. The first one has been done for you.

a) 1% of 300 $ = \frac{300}{100} = 3$

b) 1% of 1400

c) 1% of 600

d) 1% of 4500

e) 1% of 800

f) 1% of 1000

4 Calculate 1% of the following quantities. The first one has been done for you.

a) 1% of £380 $ = \frac{380}{100} = 3.8$

b) 1% of 400 litres = ❓

c) 1% of £685 = ❓

d) 1% of 4572 litres = ❓

e) 1% of £821 = ❓

f) 1% of 1599 kilometres = ❓

g) 1% of £7650 = ❓

> Don't forget to write the units in your answers.

5 Calculate 4% of each these numbers. The first two have been done for you.

a) 4% of 600 = (1% of 600) × 4

$\qquad = \frac{600}{100} \times 4$

$\qquad = 24$

b) 4% of 4300 = (1% of 4300) × 4

$\qquad = \frac{4300}{100} \times 4$

$\qquad = 43 \times 4$

$\qquad = 172$

Four per cent of a number is four times as big as one per cent.

c) 4% of 900

d) 4% of 800

e) 4% of 500

f) 4% of 1000

g) 4% of £600

h) 4% of £3200

6 Calculate the following percentages. The first two have been done for you.

a) 13% of £6100 = (1% of 6100) × 13

$\qquad = \frac{6100}{100} \times 13$

$\qquad = 61 \times 13$

$\qquad = £793$

b) 32% of 500 = (1% of 500) × 32

$\qquad = \frac{500}{100} \times 32$

$\qquad = 5 \times 32$

$\qquad = 160$

In your Maths National Test, you are most likely to find difficult calculations in Test B where you can use a calculator. If you are allowed to use a calculator, you should do so!

Some calculators have a percentage key. If yours does, you can calculate 32% of 500 by keying 32 × 500 then pressing the % key, to find the answer of 160.

c) 17% of 800

d) 18% of £250

e) 28% of £350

7 Calculate these percentages in your head.

a) 25% of 100

b) 50% of 66

c) 10% of 70

d) 100% of 6789

e) 75% of 80

f) 20% of 50

g) 50% of 86

h) 40% of 100

i) 60% of 300

It is very important that you understand how to calculate a percentage without a calculator.

Test question

Calculate **24%** of **525**.

Answers and Guidance are given on pp.44-45.

How long did you take?

12 Pie charts

What's it all about?

★ In this chapter, you will practise interpreting data from a pie chart.

★ You will need to use your knowledge of fractions and percentages.

★ In your Maths National Test, you may be asked questions about data presented as a pie chart.

> If you are not sure about fractions, look back at Book 2, Chapter 11.

1 Write what fraction of each circle has been shaded. The first one has been done for you.

a) $\frac{1}{4}$

c)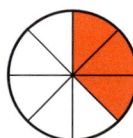

e)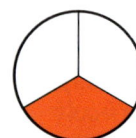

b)

d)

f)

> We can also write fractions as percentages. If you need to, look back at Chapter 6 on fractions and Chapter 11 on percentages.

2 Complete these sentences. The first one has been done for you.

a) $\frac{3}{4}$ of 100% = $\frac{3 \times 100}{4}$ = 75%

b) $\frac{1}{2}$ of 100% = ❓

c) $\frac{1}{3}$ of 100% = ❓

d) $\frac{1}{4}$ of 100% = ❓

e) $\frac{1}{8}$ of 100% = ❓

f) $\frac{1}{5}$ of 100% = ❓

g) $\frac{3}{10}$ of 100% = ❓

h) $\frac{1}{20}$ of 100% = ❓

3 This is a pie chart of favourite colours.

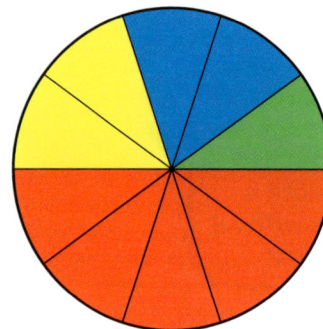

a) Copy this chart and complete it.

$\frac{1}{2}$ of the people chose red	50% of the people chose red.
$\frac{2}{10}$ or $\frac{1}{5}$ of the people chose yellow	❓ of the people chose yellow.
❓ of the people chose blue	❓ of the people chose blue.
❓ of the people chose green	❓ of the people chose green.

> You need to calculate 10% of 60 to help you. Look at Chapter 11 on percentages for help.

b) If there were 60 people altogether, how many chose each colour?

4 a) In this pie chart, $\frac{1}{4}$ of the chart represents 60 lorries. How many vehicles were there altogether?

The numbers of vehicles on a ferry

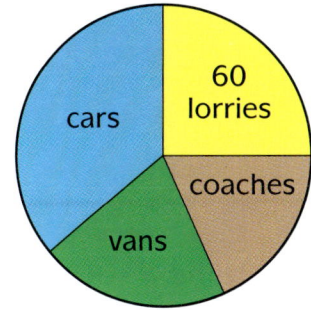

b) How many books altogether?

The numbers of books in a library

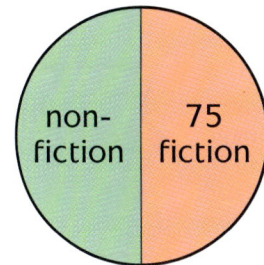

c) How many pieces of fruit altogether?

The fruit in a fruit bowl

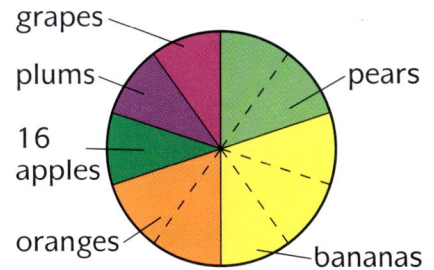

d) How many children altogether?

The numbers of children in years 4, 5 and 6

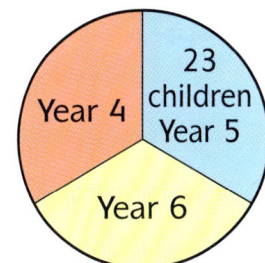

5 This is a pie chart to show favourite foods.

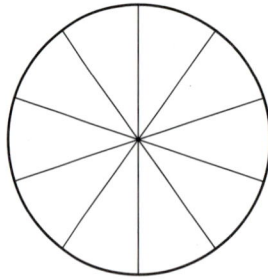

To help you the pie chart has been divided into tenths.

Copy the pie chart, then shade and label it using this information.

40% of people like pizza best.   20% of people like meat best.

25% of people like chips best.   5% of people like cheese best.

10% of people like fish best.

If there are 80 people altogether, work out how many people:

Work out what 10% of 80 is first. Working out 5% may help too.

a) like pizza best   c) like fish best   e) like cheese best.

b) like chips best   d) like meat best

Test question

This is a pie chart to show the amount of fruit a greengrocer sold in a day, in kilograms.

Fruit sold in a day

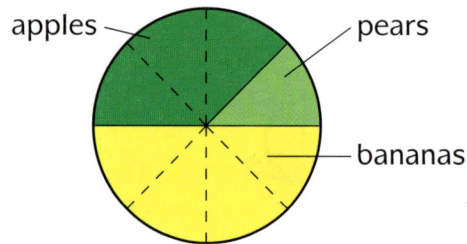

The greengrocer sold 60 kg of apples.

a) How many **pears** were sold?

b) Which type of fruit did she sell **most** of?

c) How many **kg of fruit** were sold **altogether**?

Answers and Guidance are given on p.45.

How long did you take?

🕐 *You should be able to complete these questions in 18 minutes*

1 Put these distances in order of size, starting with the **longest**:

190 centimetres

1.8 metres

1850 millimetres

✏ ....

1 mark

2 Here are four patterns.

A

B

C

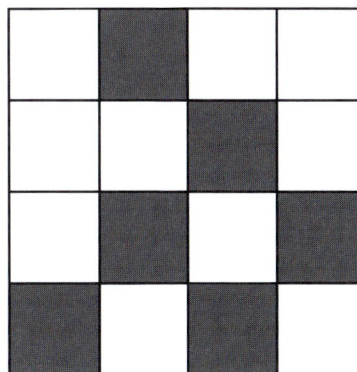

D

Put a **tick** (✓) in a box if the pattern has reflective symmetry.
Put a **cross** (✗) in a box if the pattern does not have reflective symmetry.

✏ A [ ]   B [ ]   C [ ]   D [ ]

2 marks

3 Here is a grid made of squares.

Shade **10%** of this grid.

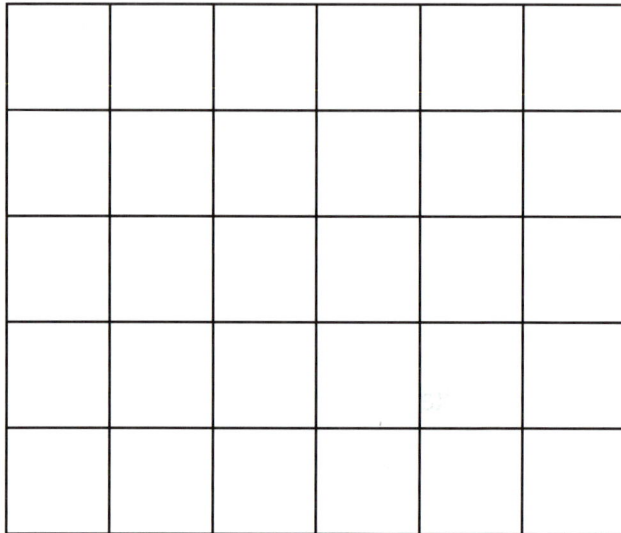

1 mark

4 This pie chart shows the percentage of people who watch EastEnders.

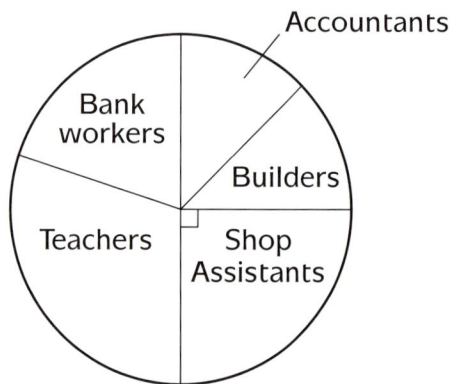

Accountants

Bank workers

Builders

Teachers

Shop Assistants

Estimate the percentage of people in each of these categories who watch the programme.

Teachers	30%
Builders	
Shop assistants	
Accountants	12.5%
Bank workers	

2 marks

5 This chart shows the types of socks worn on one school day.

There are 35 girls.

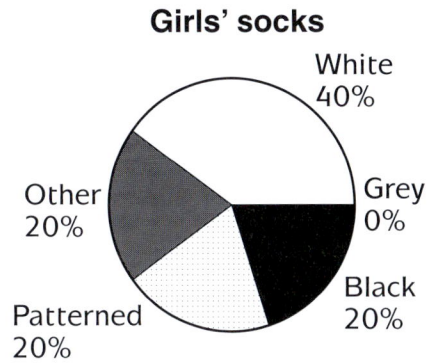

Girls' socks

White
40%

Other
20%

Grey
0%

Black
20%

Patterned
20%

Show your working. You may get a mark.

40% of the 35 girls wore white socks.

Work out how many of the girls wore white socks.

girls

2 marks

6 There are **12 pencils** in a box.

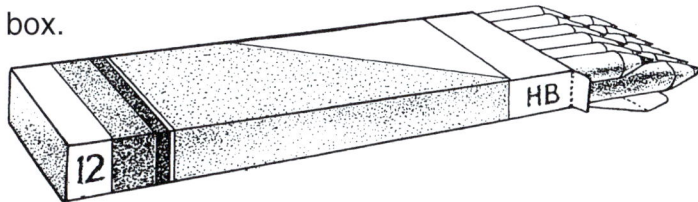

A school buys **24 boxes**.

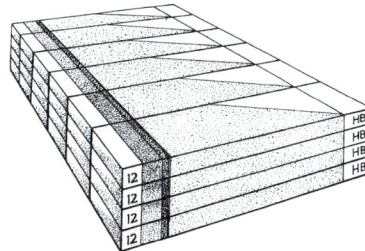

Show your working. You may get a mark.

How many **pencils** does the school buy?

Do **not** use a calculator.

pencils

2 marks

7   Here is a flag.

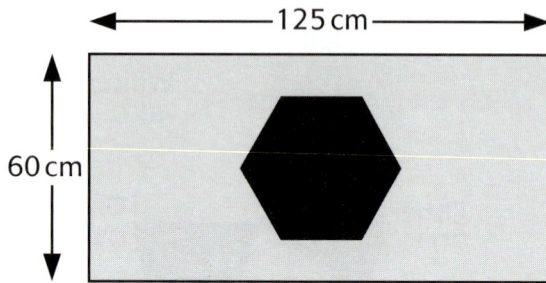

You may use a calculator.

What is the area of this flag?

cm²

1 mark

20% of the flag is blue.

What area of the flag is blue?

cm²

1 mark

Answers and Guidance are given on pp.47-48.   How long did you take?

36

Answers and Guidance

1 Multiplication and division by 10, 100, 1000 ...

This work is at level 4. It leads on to work at level 5 on conversion of metric units, covered in Book 4.

1 a) (ii) **970**   (iii) **2520**   (iv) **11030**   (v) **134650**
b) (ii) **68**   (iii) **114**   (iv) **156**   (v) **1268**
c) (ii) **75.2**   (iii) **122.4**   (iv) **146.3**   (v) **1216.4**

If any of your answers were wrong, did you remember:
- to include a zero to show there are no units
- that the decimal point appears to move one place to the right when you multiply by 10?

Look again at the margin note near this question.

2 a) $58 \times 10 =$ **580**   d) $1.44 \times 10 =$ **14.4**
b) **3.82** $\times 10 = 38.2$ e) **224** $\times 10 = 2240$
c) $148 \times$ **10** $= 1480$ f) **2.42** $\times 10 = 24.2$

3 a) ii) **3800**   iii) **9400**   iv) **21800**   v) **34600**
b) ii) **1654**   iii) **1402**   iv) **11304**   v) **110002**
c) ii) **2800.2**   iii) **34001.3**   iv) **6240**   v) **7809**

If any of your answers were wrong, did you remember:
- to put a zero where there were no units and a zero where there were no tens
- to put a zero to show there were no units when you were multiplying the numbers with only one place of decimals
- that the decimal point appears to move two places to the right when you multiply by 100? The margin note near the question explains why.

4 a) **64** $\times 100 = 6400$
b) **411** $\times 100 = 41100$
c) $100 \times$ **1481** $= 148100$
d) **6.1598** $\times 100 = 615.98$

5 a) **38400**   c) **1472300**   e) **43474**
b) **46083**   d) **2340600**   f) **2420**

If any of your answers were wrong, did you:
- multiply by the right number
- use zeros in the right places when there were no units or tens?

6 c) **18**   e) **1.374**   g) **23.24**   i) **0.1135**
d) **1.38**   f) **1.037**   h) **0.2604**

7 a) $246 \div 100 =$ **2.46**
b) $1246 \div$ **100** $= 12.46$
c) $140 \div 10 =$ **14**
d) **348.5** $\div 100 = 3.485$
e) **250** $\div 10 = 25$
f) $2358 \div 100 =$ **23.58**
g) **64210** $\div 10 = 6421$
h) $26345 \div$ **100** $= 263.45$
i) **35** $\div 100 = 0.35$

If any of your answers were wrong, did you:
- divide by the correct number
- put the decimal point in the right place
- put in zeros where they were needed?

8 a) **800** jelly beans
b) **15** sweets
c) **24.8** cm
d) **1340** km
e) **225** metres
f) **24.536** cl
g) **£236.46**

If your answers to any of these were wrong, did you:
- correctly identify whether you needed to multiply or divide
- divide or multiply by the correct number
- put in the correct number of zeros
- put the decimal point in the correct place?

Test question

I can travel **3346.02** metres on 1 litre of fuel.

I can drive **3.34602** kilometres per litre.

Target time for all questions: **35–45 minutes**

Your time for all questions

2 Probability

This chapter builds on the work on Probability in Book 1, Chapter 7 Probability.

1 **6 sections**

2 a) $\frac{1}{8}$ b) $\frac{2}{8}$ or $\frac{1}{4}$ c) $\frac{3}{8}$

If any of your answers were wrong, look back at Book 2, Chapter 11 Fractions.

3 b) **0**   **Reason:** There is no number 5 on the spinner.

Did you notice the margin note? You must write a probability as a number to get a mark.

c) $\frac{1}{8}$ **Reason:** There are eight sections on the spinner (possible outcomes), but only one of them is a 3.

d) $\frac{4}{8}$ or $\frac{1}{2}$ **Reason:** There are eight sections on the spinner (possible outcomes) and the number 2 or 4 is on four of them.

e) $\frac{4}{8}$ or $\frac{1}{2}$ **Reason:** There are eight sections on the spinner (possible outcomes), four of them have odd numbers.

4 a) **same** c) **smaller** e) **same**
  b) **larger** d) **larger** f) **smaller**

If you had difficulty with these, did you understand how to compare fractions? If not, look back at Book 2, Chapter 11 equivalent fractions.

5 a) $\frac{2}{6}$ or $\frac{1}{3}$ **Reason:** There are six sections on the spinner. Two of them have a 3 on them so there are two chances of spinning a 3.

  b) **Yes** **Reason:** On spinner A the probability of spinning a 3 is $\frac{2}{6}$ (six sections on the spinner, two of them with a 3 on them). $\frac{2}{6} = \frac{1}{3}$. On spinner B the probability is $\frac{1}{3}$ (three sections, one with a 3 on it).

  c) **Spinner A** **Reason:** On spinner A there is a $\frac{3}{6}$ chance (six sections, three with 2 on them), $\frac{3}{6} = \frac{1}{2}$. On spinner B there is a $\frac{1}{3}$ chance (three sections, one with a 2 on). $\frac{1}{2}$ is bigger than $\frac{1}{3}$ so there is more chance on spinner A.

  d) **Spinner B** **Reason:** On spinner A there is a $\frac{1}{6}$ chance of spinning a 1 (six sections, one with a 1 on it). On spinner B there is a $\frac{1}{3}$ chance of spinning a 1 (three sections, one with a 1 on it). $\frac{1}{3}$ is bigger than $\frac{1}{6}$ so there is more chance of spinning a 1 on spinner B.

When answering questions comparing probabilities a mathematical explanation (one with numbers) is sufficient, so you do not need to write the parts of the explanations given inside the brackets.

You may need to ask an adult to check your explanations. The way we have shown you to write an explanation is very clear. Look carefully at the explanations and try to learn how to word them like this. You will need to do this in your Maths National Test.

6 This is one solution. The numbers on your spinner may not be in the same order as the numbers on this spinner. Check that your spinner has eight sections:
one with a 6
two with a 2
three with a 4
two with an 8.

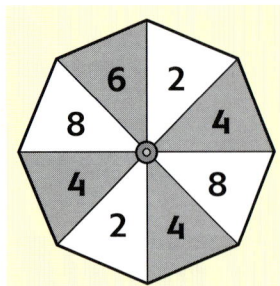

Target time for all questions: 30–40 minutes

Your time for all questions

3 Multiplying larger numbers

This chapter builds on multiplication at level 4, working towards level 5.

1 c) **9** hundreds, **7** tens, **2** units
  d) **4** hundreds, **5** tens, **2** units
  e) **8** hundreds, **9** tens, **5** units
  f) **6** hundreds, **7** tens, **4** units
  g) **7** hundreds, **5** tens, **0** units
  h) **5** hundreds, **0** tens, **3** units

2

c)
$$\begin{array}{r} 68 \\ \times\,7 \\ \hline 7 \times 8 \quad 56 \\ 7 \times 60 \quad 420 \\ \hline \mathbf{476} \end{array}$$

f)
$$\begin{array}{r} 36 \\ \times\,5 \\ \hline 5 \times 6 \quad 30 \\ 5 \times 30 \quad 150 \\ \hline \mathbf{180} \end{array}$$

d)
$$\begin{array}{r} 82 \\ \times\,8 \\ \hline 8 \times 2 \quad 16 \\ 8 \times 80 \quad 640 \\ \hline \mathbf{656} \end{array}$$

g)
$$\begin{array}{r} 71 \\ \times\,8 \\ \hline 8 \times 1 \quad 8 \\ 8 \times 70 \quad 560 \\ \hline \mathbf{568} \end{array}$$

e)
$$\begin{array}{r} 76 \\ \times\,9 \\ \hline 9 \times 6 \quad 54 \\ 9 \times 70 \quad 630 \\ \hline \mathbf{684} \end{array}$$

h)
$$\begin{array}{r} 89 \\ \times\,6 \\ \hline 6 \times 9 \quad 54 \\ 6 \times 80 \quad 480 \\ \hline \mathbf{534} \end{array}$$
1.

When you are confident you can multiply like this:

2 c)
$$\begin{array}{r} 68 \\ \times\,7 \\ \hline \mathbf{476} \\ 5 \end{array}$$

d)
$$\begin{array}{r} 82 \\ \times\,8 \\ \hline \mathbf{656} \\ 1 \end{array}$$

e)
$$\begin{array}{r} 76 \\ \times\,9 \\ \hline \mathbf{684} \\ 5 \end{array}$$

Answers and Guidance

f)
```
    36
  ×  5
  ─────
   180
     3
```

g)
```
    71
  ×  8
  ─────
   568
```

h)
```
    89
  ×  6
  ─────
   534
     5
```

If any of your answers were wrong, check that:
- you know your tables and multiplied correctly (look at Book 1, Chapter 5 Using multiplication if you need more practice)
- you remembered when you were multiplying units and when you were multiplying tens
- when you multiplied by ten you put a zero in the units column
- you carried out your addition correctly.
- if you wrote the examples as a single sum, you carried from the units to the tens, adding on correctly.

3 c) **938**   e) **3681**   g) **6288**
    d) **4608**   f) **1635**   h) **5832**

If any of your answers were wrong, look at the guidance for question 2.

Check that you understand how to multiply hundreds correctly, and that when multiplying by hundreds, you put a zero in the units column and a zero in the tens column.

4 c) **1961**   e) **2691**   g) **3408**
    d) **8148**   f) **4760**   h) **6138**

If any of your answers were wrong, check:
- your multiplication and addition, making sure that you carried and added in the carried numbers correctly
- that you remembered the zero in the units column when multiplying by ten.

5 c) **5530**   e) **17894**   g) **75894**
    d) **6408**   f) **43699**   h) **50967**

6 a) 144 × 26 = **3744** bags of sweets
    b) 76 × 52 = **3952** supporters
    c) 846 × 24 = **20304** eggs

Remember to write down the units in which you are giving your answer.

Test question

```
     431
   ×  23
  ──────
    1293
    8620
  ──────
    9913
```

Target time for all questions: 40–50 minutes

Your time for all questions

4 Nets

This chapter contains work at level 4.

2 a) Its faces are **square**.
    b) It has **six** faces.
    c) It has **eight** vertices.
    d) It has **twelve** edges.

3 a) A **cube**.
    b) Ask an adult to check your results. Not all the nets you could have made will fold into a cube.

4 a) A **square** and a **triangle**.
    b) A square-based pyramid has **five** faces.

If you are unsure of any definitions, look back at Book 2, Chapters 1 and 10 on Properties of shape.

5 You should have made a **triangular prism**.

If you did not, check your measurements and try again.

Test question

A, **C** and **D** fold into an open box.

If you did not get this right, try drawing the shapes on paper and folding them.

Target time for all questions: 45–55 minutes

Your time for all questions

5 Negative numbers

This chapter contains work on negative numbers at level 5.

1 b) −35   −11   −9   −8   −2   3   9
    c) −4   −3   −1   2   4   6   9
    d) −9   −2   −1   0   3   6   8
    e) −94   −89   −58   0   98   100   111

If any of your answers were wrong, did you:
- remember that your sequence had to begin with the 'largest' negative number, the next 'largest' negative number, and so on
- draw a number line to help you?

2 b) **−8**   d) **−36**   f) **−104**
    c) **−34**   e) **−44**

If any of your answers were wrong, did you:
- draw a number line to help you
- calculate or count back accurately?

Answers and Guidance

3 b) 18 **12** 6 0 **−6** **−12** −18
c) 15 10 **5** **0** **−5** −10 **−15** **−20**
d) 22 13 **4** −5 **−14** **−23** −32
e) 11 7 **3** **−1** **−5** −9 **−13** **−17**

If any of your answers were wrong, did you:
● subtract the correct amount in each sequence
● use a number line if you had difficulty?

4 b)

c)

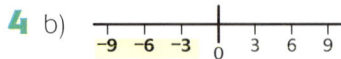

d)

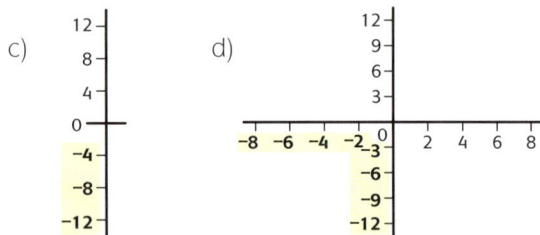

If any of your answers were wrong, did you:
● work out what scale was being used on each axis
● subtract accurately?

5 a) **13** degrees, from 3°C to −10°C
b) **7** degrees, from −1°C to −8°C
c) **−50** metres, −40 + 5 − 15
d) **32** metres, −100 up to −68

If any of your answers were wrong, did you:
● work out what mathematics you needed to use to solve the problem
● use a number line to help you if you had difficulty?

6 a) **72** m   b) **44** m   c) **62** m

7 a) **Saturday**: sales 132   c) **29** papers
b) **Tuesday**: sales 84   d) **+48** (over target)

If any of your answers to questions 6 or 7 were wrong, did you:
● write out a chart as suggested
● remember to subtract from 60 each time in question 6
● subtract from 100 each day in question 7?

Test question

a) **10 degrees**
b) **−4°C**

If either of your answers was wrong, did you:
● use a number line to work out the differences
● use the correct numbers from the chart?

Target time for all questions: **50–60 minutes**

Your time for all questions

6 Fractions

This chapter builds on work on fractions covered in Book 2, Chapter 11 Fractions. The work is at level 4.

1 3

2 c) 6 ÷ 3 = **2**   e) 12 ÷ 6 = **2**   g) 10 ÷ 10 = **1**
d) 20 ÷ 5 = **4**   f) 24 ÷ 8 = **3**   h) 18 ÷ 9 = **2**

3 a) **14**   c) **16**   e) **23**   g) **33**
b) **15**   d) **26**   f) **17**   h) **21**

4 c) $\frac{2}{8}$ of 56 = 2 × 7 = **14**
d) $\frac{3}{5}$ of 75 = 3 × 15 = **45**
e) $\frac{4}{9}$ of 63 = 4 × 7 = **28**
f) $\frac{3}{4}$ × 80 = 3 × 20 = **60**
g) $\frac{2}{6}$ × 108 = 2 × 18 = **36**
h) $\frac{6}{10}$ × 130 = 6 × 13 = **78**

If any of your answers were wrong, did you:
● divide the number by the denominator (the bottom part of the fraction) and multiply by the numerator
● calculate carefully – or use a calculator correctly?

5 c) $\frac{16}{32} = \frac{2}{4} = \frac{1}{2}$ g) $\frac{36}{48} = \frac{6}{8} = \frac{3}{4}$
d) $\frac{60}{100} = \frac{6}{10} = \frac{3}{5}$ h) $\frac{36}{72} = \frac{3}{6} = \frac{1}{2}$
e) $\frac{30}{50} = \frac{3}{5}$ i) $\frac{50}{100} = \frac{5}{10} = \frac{1}{2}$
f) $\frac{12}{42} = \frac{2}{7}$ j) $\frac{28}{35} = \frac{4}{5}$

There are several different ways of reducing some of these fractions. Even if you did it another way, you should still have ended up with the same answer. If you did not, check your arithmetic, or ask a grown up to look at the method you have used.

6 c) 12 is $\frac{12}{36}$ of 36 $\frac{12}{36} = \frac{1}{3}$
d) 2 is $\frac{2}{18}$ of 18 $\frac{2}{18} = \frac{1}{9}$
e) 16 is $\frac{16}{24}$ of 24 $\frac{16}{24} = \frac{2}{3}$
f) 20 is $\frac{20}{30}$ of 30 $\frac{20}{30} = \frac{2}{3}$
g) 35 is $\frac{35}{50}$ of 50 $\frac{35}{50} = \frac{7}{10}$
h) 27 is $\frac{27}{36}$ of 36 $\frac{27}{36} = \frac{3}{4}$

7 b) $\frac{1}{5}$ of 35 = 7   So **7** children are away.
c) $\frac{1}{4}$ × 40 = 10   Sam gives his friend **10** sweets.
d) $\frac{21}{28} = \frac{3}{4}$ $\frac{3}{4}$ of the books are returned.
e) $\frac{1}{7}$ × 21 = 3   These are **3** bananas.

If any of your answers were wrong, check:
● that you understood which mathematics you had to do to solve the problem
● your arithmetic.

Answers and Guidance

Target time for all questions: 35–45 minutes

Your time for all questions

7 Missing numbers

This chapter contains work at level 4 which involves inverse operations.

e.g. $624 \div 39 = 16$ and $16 \times 39 = 624$

To achieve the next level, level 5, you must be able to apply this knowledge to check solutions to number problems.

1 a) **3**   b) **21**   c) **7**   d) **21**

2 a) **6**   b) **18**   c) **3**   d) **18**

3 a) $18 \div 9 = $ **2**   c) $18 \div $ **2** $ = $ **9**
      b) $9 \times $ **2** $ = 18$ d) **2** $ \times $ **9** $ = 18$

If any of your answers to questions 1, 2 or 3 were wrong, check that you:

- started with the right number, divided them equally and wrote the number of groups
- know your multiplication tables.

4 b)   10
        $10 \div 5 = 2$
        $10 \div 2 = 5$
        $5 \times 2 \ = 10$
        $2 \times 5 \ = 10$

   c)   56
        $56 \div 7 = 8$
        $56 \div 8 = 7$
        $7 \times 8 \ = 56$
        $8 \times 7 \ = 56$

   d)   27
        $27 \div 3 = 9$
        $27 \div 9 = 3$
        $3 \times 9 \ = 27$
        $9 \times 3 \ = 27$

   e)   45
        $45 \div 9 = 5$
        $45 \div 5 = 9$
        $9 \times 5 \ = 45$
        $5 \times 9 \ = 45$

   f)   42
        $42 \div 7 = 6$
        $42 \div 6 = 7$
        $7 \times 6 \ = 42$
        $6 \times 7 \ = 42$

If any of your answers were wrong:

- try out the process explained in question 1 with each number in question 4

  For example, take 10 objects, divide them into 5 groups ($10 \div 5$). How many in each group? Put them together again (5×2). Now divide your 10 objects into 2 groups ($10 \div 2$). How many in each group? Put them together again (2×5).

- check your tables again!

5 a) $276 \times 35 = 9660$
      $35 \times 276 = $ **9660**
      $9660 \div 35 = $ **276**
      $9660 \div 276 = $ **35**

   b) $31 \times 42 = 1302$
      $42 \times 31 = $ **1302**
      $1302 \div 31 = $ **42**
      $1302 \div 42 = $ **31**

   c) $26 \times 91 = $ **2366**
      $91 \times 26 = $ **2366**
      $2366 \div 91 = $ **26**
      $2366 \div 26 = $ **91**

6 a) $379 \times 27 = $ **10 233**
      $27 \times 379 = $ **10 233**
      $10 233 \div 27 = $ **379**
      $10 233 \div 379 = $ **27**

   b) $163 \times 59 = $ **9617**
      $59 \times 163 = $ **9617**
      $9617 \div 59 = $ **163**
      9617 $ \div 163 = $ **59**

   c) $228 \times 91 = $ **20 748**
      $91 \times 228 = $ **20 748**
      $20 748 \div 91 = $ **228**
      $20 748 \div $ **228** $ = $ **91**

7 a) $33 \times 356 = $ **11 748**
      356 $ \times 33 = $ **11 748**
      11 748 $ \div 33 = $ **356**
      $11 748 \div $ **356** $ = $ **33**

   b) $24 \times 192 = $ **4608**
      192 $ \times 24 = $ **4608**
      4608 $ \div 24 = $ **192**
      4608 $ \div 192 = $ **24**

   c) $42 \times 220 = $ **9240**
      220 $ \times 42 = $ **9240**
      9240 $ \div 42 = $ **220**
      9240 $ \div 220 = $ **42**

   d) $267 \times 28 = $ **7476**
      28 $ \times 267 = 7476$
      7476 $ \div 28 = 267$
      $7476 \div 267 = 28$

   e) $9212 \div 14 = $ **658**
      $9212 \div $ **658** $ = 14$
      658 $ \times 14 = 9212$
      $14 \times $ **658** $ = 9212$

   f) $14 364 \div 19 = $ **756**
      14 364 $ \div $ **756** $ = 19$
      19 $ \times $ **756** $ = $ **14 364**
      756 $ \times 19 = $ **14 364**

If any of your answers were wrong in this section, look back at question 5 and see how the pattern of the numbers is repeated. Notice how the largest number is made by multiplying the other two and how the other numbers are found.

8 b) **Working:** $3026 \div 34 = 89$
       Answer: **89** $ \times 34 = 3026$

   c) **Working:** $1352 \div 52 = 26$
      Answer: $1352 \div $ **52** $ = 26$

   d) **Working:** $1065 \div 71 = 15$
      Answer: $1065 \div $ **15** $ = 71$

9 a) $21 845 \div $ **257** $ = 85$
   b) $16 029 \div $ **39** $ = 411$
   c) $51 142 \div $ **562** $ = 91$
   d) $8924 \div $ **46** $ = 194$

Answers and Guidance

Test question

$10\,233 \div 27 = 379$

Target time for all questions: 40–50 minutes

Your time for all questions

8 Area and perimeter

This chapter builds on work on perimeter in Book 1, Chapter 8 Perimeters and on area in Book 2, Chapter 5 Area. It contains work at levels 4 and 5.

1 a) **12** cm²   b) **14** cm²   c) **5** cm²

If any of your answers were wrong, look back at Book 2, Chapter 5.

2 b) **45** cm²   d) **400** cm²   f) **45** cm²
   c) **48** m²   e) **32** m²

If any of your answers were wrong, did you:
- use the formula and multiply the base measurement by the height for each rectangle
- multiply correctly?

3 a) **19** cm   b) **20** cm   c) **20** cm

You were only given one measurement in shape (c) because the shape is a square, all the sides are the same length.

If any of your answers were wrong, look back at Book 1, Chapter 8 Perimeters.

4 b) **5** cm²   c) **$7\frac{1}{2}$** cm²   d) **$7\frac{1}{2}$** cm²

If any of your answers were wrong, did you pair up the triangles and count in whole squares as far as possible?

Try again, this time mark the squares as you pair them up and count them.

5 b) **20** cm²   c) **42** cm²   d) **27** cm²

If any of your answers were wrong, did you remember to multiply the measurements and then divide by two?

6 a) **100** cm²   c) **112.5** cm²
   b) **62.5** cm²   d) **187.5** cm²

If any of your answers were wrong, did you:
- work out that the area of one square was 25 cm² (5 × 5)
- work out the area of a triangle was 12.5 cm²
- add the areas correctly?
Check again!

Test question

Area **84** m²

If your answer was wrong, did you:
- count the whole rectangles
- count the half rectangles (triangles) and make two whole rectangles
- multiply 12 × 7 correctly?

Target time for all questions: 25–30 minutes

Your time for all questions

9 Conversion of units

1 1 metre (m) = **100** centimetres (cm)
1 metre = **1000** millimetres (mm)
1 kilometre (km) = **1000** metres

If you do not know these, you need to learn them.

2 1 kilometre = **100 000** centimetres
(1000 m = 1000 × 100 cm)
1 kilometre = **1 000 000** millimetres
(1000 m = 1000 × 100 cm = 100 000 × 10 mm)
1 metre = **1000** millimetres
(1 m = 100 cm = 100 × 10 mm)
1 centimetre = **10** millimetres

If any of your answers were wrong, did you multiply correctly by the right number? Look again at your table in question 1 and at Chapter 1 Multiplication by 10, 100 and 1000.

3 1000 grams (g) = **1** kilogram (kg)
1 litre (l) = **100** centilitres (cl)
1 litre = **1000** millilitres (ml)
1 centilitre = **10** millilitres

If you do not know these, you need to learn them.

4 a) **metres**
b) **kilometres**
c) **grams**
d) **kilograms**
e) depending on size: small insects **millimetres**, larger insects **centimetres**
f) **centimetres**
g) **centilitres** or **millilitres**
h) **millilitres**

If you have problems with the size of these units, look around you; in your kitchen cupboard, at the supermarket, when you are cooking, going for a drive or getting petrol. You need to get a feel for the size of each unit.

Answers and Guidance

5 b) 2.46 kg = **2460** g
c) £4.28 = **428** pence
d) 27.92 l = **2792** cl
e) 135 m = **13 500** cm
f) 9.5 km = **9500** m
g) 15.64 cm = **156.4** mm
h) 87.6 cl = **876** ml
i) 4.78 l = **4780** ml

Did you work out correctly what you had to multiply *by* each time?

6 b) 325 cm = **3.25** m   e) 895 ml = **89.5** cl
c) 264 cl = **2.64** l   g) 2423 m = **2.423** km
d) 1476 g = **1.476** kg   h) 1212 mm = **121.2** cm
f) 3116 ml = **3.116** l   i) 1714 ml = **1.714** l

Did you work out correctly what number you had to divide *by* each time?

7 a) 671p = £**6.71**   f) 659 ml = **65.9** cl
b) 15.86 kg = **15 860** g   g) 17.53 cm = **175.3** mm
c) £13.99 = **1399** pence h) 75.8 cl = **758** ml
d) 9864 g = **9.864** kg   i) 56.3 l = **56 300** ml
e) 5935 ml = **5.935** l

Did you:
- work out correctly whether to multiply or divide each time
- know how much to multiply or divide by? If not look back at the tables in questions 1, 2 and 3.

8 **mass:** *imperial*: pound, ounce, *metric*: kilogram, gram
length: *imperial*: mile, foot, inch, yard, *metric*: metre, kilometre, centimetre, millimetre
capacity: *imperial*: gallon, pint, *metric*: litre, millilitre
time: *imperial*: minute, hour, day, year
metric: century, millennium, decade, second

If any of your answers were wrong, look in a dictionary to check the meaning of the words and then learn them.

9 b) **smaller**   d) **lighter**   f) **longer**
c) **heavier**   e) **longer**   g) **shorter**

10 **mass:** kilogram, pound, ounce, gram
length: mile, kilometre, metre, yard, foot, inch, centimetre, millimetre
capacity: gallon, litre, pint, millilitre
time: millennium, century, decade, year, day, hour, minute, second

If any of your answers were wrong, look back at the various pieces of information you have been given. Ask an adult to help you. You need to get a feel for the relative size of units by the activities suggested in question 4.

10 Reflective symmetry

This chapter builds on Book 1, Chapter 11 Reflective symmetry. It contains work on reflection at level 4.

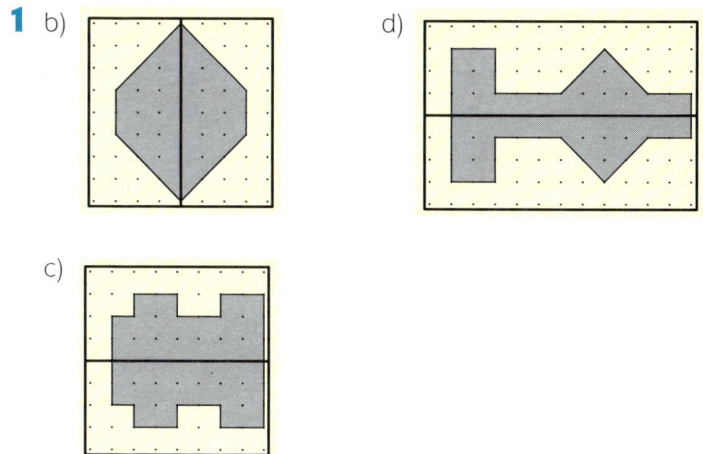

1 b)   d)

c)

If any of your answers were wrong, did you count the dots and draw your shape carefully?
Look back to Book 1, Chapter 11 Reflective symmetry for more practice.

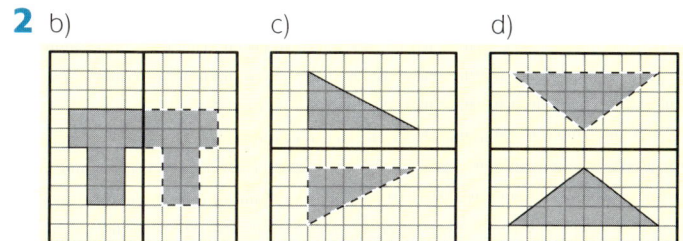

2 b)   c)   d)

If any of your answers were wrong, see the guidance above.

Answers and Guidance

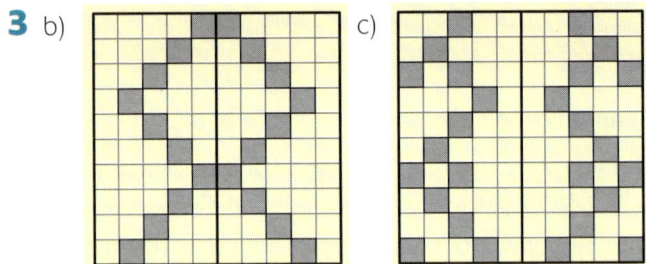

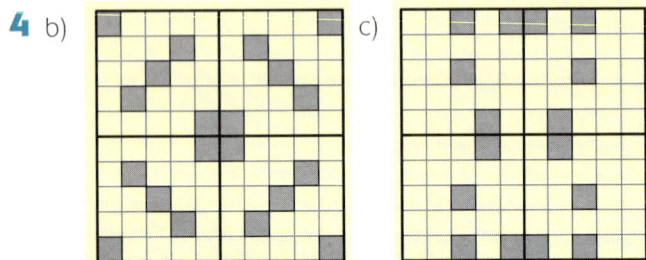

3 b) c)

4 b) c)

If any of your answers in questions 3 and 4 were wrong, see the guidance above and think:
- did you see whether the shape 'looks' correct
- is the shape you have drawn symmetrical
- is it a reflection of the shapes in other quadrants?

Test question

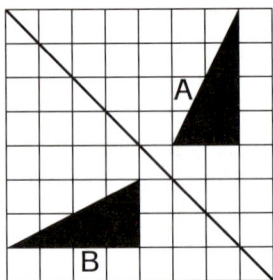

Shape **B** is a reflection of Shape A.

If your answer was wrong, did you:
- attempt to draw in mirror lines between the triangles
- see that only B could be a reflection of A?

🕐 **Target time for all questions: 25–35 minutes**

🕐 **Your time for all questions**

11 Percentages

1 a) $\frac{1}{2}$ = **50%**

b) $\frac{1}{4}$ = **25%**

c) $\frac{3}{4}$ = **75%**

d) 1 = **100%**

If you got any of these wrong, you need to look carefully at the diagram.

For instance, notice that $\frac{3}{4}$ of the circle was covered by the parts marked 50% and 25%, so $\frac{3}{4}$ = 25% and 50% = 75%.

2 $\frac{1}{10}$ = 0.1 = **10**%

$\frac{5}{10}$ = 0.5 = **50**%

$\frac{3}{10}$ = **0.3** = **30**%

$\frac{7}{10}$ = **0.7** = **70**%

If any of your answers were wrong, use the diagram to help.

If you know that $\frac{1}{10}$ = 0.1 = 10%, all the rest of the answers can be found by counting the sections and multiplying.

3 b) **14**

c) **6**

d) **45**

e) **8**

f) **10**

If you had difficulty, make sure you understand that $1\% = \frac{1}{100}$ and that you need to divide by 100 each time. For help with this, look at Chapter 1 Multiplication by 10, 100, 1000….

4 b) **4** litres

c) **£6.85**

d) **45.72** litres

e) **£8.21**

f) **15.99** kilometres

g) **£76.50**

Did you:
- remember the units
- remember that you must write a zero in the pence column when you are writing money (£76.50)
- divide by 100 correctly?

5 c) **36**

d) **32**

e) **20**

f) **40**

g) **£24**

h) **£128**

If you got any wrong, check you understand that to calculate 4% you have first to divide by 100, then multiply by 4.

6 c) **136**

d) **£45**

e) **£98**

Did you:
- calculate 1% by dividing by 100 and then find the required percentage by multiplying correctly
- remember the units?

Answers and Guidance

7 a) **25**
b) **33**
c) **7**
d) **6789**
e) **60**
f) **10**
g) **43**
h) **40**
i) **180**

If any of your answers were wrong, you need to think again about what percentages mean. Look back at the diagrams for questions 1 and 2.

Test question

126

1% of 525 = 5.25

24% = 24 × 5.25 = 126

⏱ Target time for all questions: **45–55 minutes**

⏱ Your time for all questions

12 Pie charts

This chapter builds on work in Book 1, Chapter 9 Bar graphs and Book 2, Chapter 9 Line graphs. It also uses knowledge of fractions and percentages covered in this book. This chapter is working towards level 5.

1 b) $\frac{1}{2}$ c) $\frac{3}{8}$ d) $\frac{1}{8}$ e) $\frac{1}{3}$ f) $\frac{1}{10}$

2 b) $\frac{1}{2}$ of 100% = **50%**

c) $\frac{1}{3}$ of 100% = **$33\frac{1}{3}$%** or **$33.\dot{3}$%**

d) $\frac{1}{4}$ of 100% = **25%**

e) $\frac{1}{8}$ of 100% = **12.5%** (or **$12\frac{1}{2}$%**)

f) $\frac{1}{5}$ of 100% = **20%**

g) $\frac{3}{10}$ of 100% = **30%**

h) $\frac{1}{20}$ of 100% = **5%**

If any of your answers for these percentages were wrong did you:
● divide 100 by the denominator (the bottom) of the fraction
● then multiply by the numerator (the top)?

3 a)

$\frac{1}{2}$ of the people chose red	50% of people chose red
$\frac{2}{10}$ or $\frac{1}{5}$ of the people chose yellow	**20%** of the people chose yellow
$\frac{2}{10}$ or $\frac{1}{5}$ of the people chose blue	**20%** of the people chose blue
$\frac{1}{10}$ of the people chose green	**10%** of the people chose green

b) **30** chose red, **12** chose yellow, **12** chose blue and **6** chose green.

If your answers to these were wrong, did you:
● divide 60 by 10 to find our how many people equalled 10% (6)
● then work out the answers from there?

4 a) **240** vehicles   c) **160** pieces of fruit
b) **150** books   d) **69** children

5 Your pie chart may not look exactly like this but you should have 4 divisions for pizza, 2 divisions for meat, 1 division for fish, $2\frac{1}{2}$ divisions for chips and $\frac{1}{2}$ division for cheese.

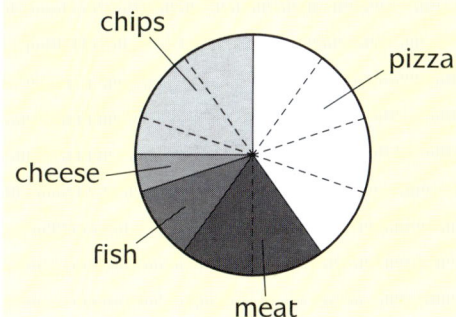

a) **32**   b) **20**   c) **8**   d) **16**   e) **4**

If you did not get these answers, did you:
● divide 80 by 10 to find out how many people equalled 10% (8)
● then work out the answers from there?

Test question

a) **20 kg pears**
b) **bananas**
c) **160 kg of fruit were sold**

If your answer was wrong, did you work out that:
● apples made up $\frac{3}{8}$ and 60 kg of the whole were sold
● pears made up $\frac{1}{8}$ or 12% so 20 kg were sold
● there were 8 × 20 kg of fruit sold altogether?

⏱ Target time for all questions: **35–45 minutes**

⏱ Your time for all questions

Answers and Guidance

1 200

If your answer was wrong, did you remember that when you divide by 10 you 'lose' a zero and therefore that the missing number must be 200?

CROSS-CHECK	**CHAPTER 1** Multiplication and division by 10, 100, 1000 …

2 $\frac{1}{8}$

Spinner B

Lee has a $\frac{3}{8}$ chance of getting a 1 on spinner A.

He has a $\frac{2}{4}$ chance of getting a 1 on spinner B.

$\frac{2}{4} = \frac{1}{2}$ and is bigger than $\frac{3}{8}$, so Lee is more likely to get a 1 on spinner B.

CROSS-CHECK	**CHAPTER 2** Probability

3 £80.50

For this question you need to do two multiplication sums:

$$£23.00 \times 2 = £46.00$$

$$£11.50 \times 3 = £34.50$$

and then add the two answers together.

£46.00 + £34.50 = £80.50

If you had difficulty, did you:
- read the question carefully and multiply the correct numbers together
- do the multiplication correctly
- remember that you were multiplying money and that you needed to put a zero after the 5 in £80.50?

CROSS-CHECK	**CHAPTER 3** Multiplying larger numbers

4 There are six different possible solutions to this question.

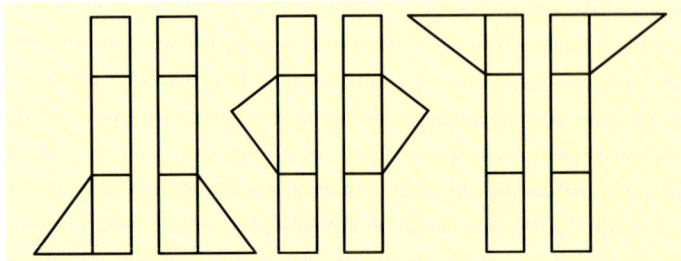

The first solution is the easiest to understand. Here are the steps you need to take.

1. Identify one face which is missing – it is triangular.
2. Make a rough sketch of this face – put in its measurements.

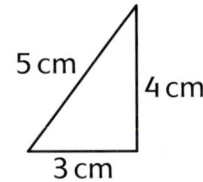

5 cm / 4 cm / 3 cm

3. Match your rough sketch to the partly-drawn net – use the measurements to decide where it needs to go.
4. Now draw this missing shape onto the net. Use a protractor to make the right angle, and a ruler to measure the correct lengths of the horizontal side (3 cm).

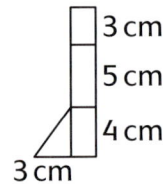

3 cm / 5 cm / 4 cm / 3 cm

5. Complete the triangle by drawing the diagonal (this is 5 cm long).

If you are still having difficulty with nets, collect lots of different shaped boxes and undo the edges to have a look at the shape of the nets.

CROSS-CHECK	**CHAPTER 4** Nets

Answers and Guidance

National Test Questions 2

1 You should have circled **–5** and **3**, or **–4** and **4**, or **–3** and **5**.

If your answer to this question was wrong, did you use the numbers as a number line and count to find a difference of eight between two numbers?

CROSS-CHECK   **CHAPTER 5** Negative numbers

2

Class	Number of children in the class	Fraction of the children away	Number of children away
1	**33**	$\frac{2}{11}$	6
2	30	$\frac{3}{10}$	**9**
3	35	$\frac{14}{35}$ or $\frac{2}{5}$	14

If you had difficulty, did you:
- see that in Class 1 $\frac{2}{11}$ is six children so $\frac{1}{11}$ is three children and therefore $\frac{11}{11} = 3 \times 11 = 33$
- work out that in Class 2 $\frac{3}{10}$ of 30 = 3 × 3 = 9
- understand that $\frac{14}{35}$ of the class were away and that this could be simplified by dividing the top and bottom of the fraction by 7 to make $\frac{2}{5}$?

CROSS-CHECK   **CHAPTER 6** Fractions

3 **480** × 15 = 32

If your answer to this question was wrong, did you:

- remember the relationship between multiplication and division and see that the sum you had to do was 32 × 15
- do the calculation like this?

$$\begin{array}{r} 32 \\ \times\ 15 \\ \hline 160 \\ 320 \\ \hline 480 \end{array}$$

CROSS-CHECK   **CHAPTER 7** Missing numbers

CHAPTER 3 Multiplying larger numbers

4

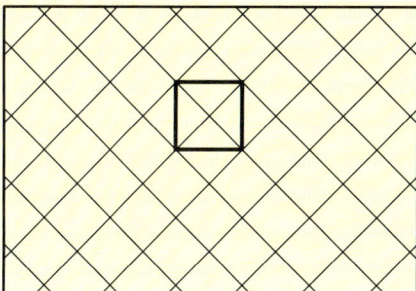

If your answer was wrong, did you:
- realise that you could not make a square with an area of 2 cm^2 using whole squares on the grid
- work out that four half-centimetre squares make two centimetre squares
- understand that squares can be divided in half diagonally?

CROSS-CHECK   **CHAPTER 8** Area and perimeter

5 $\frac{2}{10}$ or $\frac{1}{5}$

0 (or **zero**)

If your answers were wrong, did you:
- realise that there were a total of ten sides on the two dice and that two have a 1 on them
- realise that the maximum possible total is 10
- remember to write zero either as a numeral or a word?

CROSS-CHECK   **CHAPTER 2** Probability

National Test Questions 3

1 The correct order is:
190 centimetres
1850 millimetres
1.8 metres

If your answer was wrong, did you:
- convert each of the distances into either millimetres or metres so that you could compare them, like this
  either
  190 centimetres = 1.9 m
  1850 millimetres = 1.85 m
  compared with 1.8 m

  or
  190 centimetres = 190 × 10 mm = 1900 mm
  1.8 metres = 1.8 × 1000 mm = 1800 mm
  compared with 1850 mm

- See that 190 cm is the longest, then 1850 mm, then 1.8 metres?

CROSS-CHECK   **CHAPTER 9** Conversion of units

Answers and Guidance

2 A ✗   B ✓   C ✓   D ✗

If your answers were wrong, did you:
- correctly identify the possible mirror lines on each shape, i.e. the lines which divide the whole shape exactly in half
- remember a mirror line can be a diagonal as in C
- accurately judge whether the pattern on one side of the mirror line was an exact reflection of the pattern on the other side? (You have to do this for each possible mirror line, but you only need to find one accurate reflection for the pattern to have reflective symmetry.)

If you still have difficulty with these, try using a small mirror to locate any mirror lines.

CROSS-CHECK   **CHAPTER 10** Reflective symmetry

3 You should have shaded in three squares only.

If you shaded in more or less than three squares, did you:
- count the total number of squares (30) correctly
- work out 10% of 30, *either* as $\frac{30}{10} = 3$ *or* as $\frac{30}{100} \times 10 = 3$?

CROSS-CHECK   **CHAPTER 11** Percentages

4 The percentages are approximately as follows.

Teachers	30%
Builders	**12.5%**
Shop assistants	**25%**
Accountants	12.5%
Bank workers	**20%**

If you had difficulty did you see that:
- teachers and bank workers together made up 50% of the people and that as teachers were 30%, bank workers must be 20%
- accountants and builders together made up 25% of the people and that accountants were 12.5%, so builders must also be 12.5%?

CROSS-CHECK   **CHAPTER 12** Pie charts

5 **14 girls**

If your answer was wrong, did you work out 40% of 35:
- either by finding 10% and then multiplying by 4 to get 40%: $\frac{35}{10} = 3.5$ and $3.5 \times 4 = 14$
- or by finding 1% and then multiplying by 40 to get 40%: $\frac{35}{100} = 0.35$ and $0.35 \times 40 = 14$.

CROSS-CHECK   **CHAPTER 12** Pie charts

                    CHAPTER 11 Percentages

6 **288**

If you did not get this answer, check that:
- your working was correct

$$\begin{array}{r} 24 \\ \times\ 12 \\ \hline 48 \\ 240 \\ \hline 288 \end{array}$$

- you remembered that you were multiplying by 10 in the second part of your calculation and that you put a zero in the units column.

CROSS-CHECK   **CHAPTER 3** Multiplying larger numbers

7 The area of the flag is **7500 cm²**.

If you found this difficult, did you:
- remember that the area of the rectangle is obtained by multiplying the height by the length
- multiply 125 × 60 correctly, either on a calculator or on paper
$125 \times 60 = 7500$
- read the question carefully, not being put off by the shape in the middle of the flag?

CROSS-CHECK   **CHAPTER 8** Area and perimeter

                    CHAPTER 3 Multiplying larger numbers

1500 cm² of the flag is blue.

You can calculate this:
- either by calculating 10% of 7500 and multiplying by 2
$7500 \div 10 = 750$
$750 \times 2 = 1500$
- or by calculating 1% and multiplying by 20
$7500 \div 100 = 75$
$75 \times 20 = 1500$

Don't forget to put the cm² on the end of your answer – remember you are calculating an area.

CROSS-CHECK   **CHAPTER 8** Area and perimeter

                    CHAPTER 11 Percentages